# The Parent's Guide to Storytelling

# MARGARET READ MacDONALD

# The Parent's Guide to Storytelling

## How to Make Up New Stories and Retell Old Favorites

August House Publishers, Inc.
LITTLE ROCK

Printed in the United States of America
Typography by Al Cetta
Illustrations by Ted Parkhurst

10 9 8 7 6 5 4 3 2 1  HB
10 9 8 7 6 5 4 3 2 1  PB

LIBRARY OF CONGRESS CATALOGING-IN-PUBLICATION DATA

MacDonald, Margaret Read, 1940–
    The parent's guide to storytelling : how to make up new stories and
retell old favorites / Margaret Read MacDonald.—2nd ed.
      p.   cm.
    Includes bibliographical references and index.
    ISBN 0-87483-619-0 (alk. paper)—
    ISBN 0-87483-618-2 (pbk. : alk. paper)
    I. Storytelling.  2. Family recreation.  I. Title.
LB1042.M19 2001
649'.58—DC21                                  2001022116

The paper used in this publication meets the minimum requirements
of the American National Standard for Information Sciences-
Permanence of Paper for Printed Library Materials, ANSI Z39.48-1984.

AUGUST HOUSE       PUBLISHERS       LITTLE ROCK

For my father, who still tells us stories at ninety-two.

And for my daughters, Jenny and Julie,
who are telling their own stories now!

# Contents

**Why Tell Stories?**     1

**How to Tell Stories**     7

**For the Youngest Listeners**     13

  **Favorite Nursery Tales**     15
    THE THREE BEARS     15
    THE LITTLE RED HEN     18
    THE GINGERBREAD MAN     20

  **Fingerplay Stories**     24
    THE BEEHIVE     24
    FOXIE'S HOLE     24
    THE PARROT WITH THE KEY TO ROME     25
    THE LOST MITTEN     26

**Bedtime Stories, Expandable Tales, and Endless Tales**     33

  **Bedtime Stories**     35
    THE SQUEAKY DOOR     35

  **Expandable Stories**     42
    MS. MOUSE NEEDS A FRIEND     42

  **Endless Tales: The Storyteller's Exit**     48
    A DARK AND STORMY NIGHT     48
    A SILLY QUESTION     49
    THE BIRD CATCHER     49

**Easy-to-Tell Folktales**     51

  **Participation Folktales**     53
    CHEESE AND CRACKERS     53

Folktales with Many Variants    62
   STRONGEST ONE OF ALL    62
Story Stretches    67
   LET'S GO ON A BEAR HUNT!    67
Drawing Stories    71
   THE STORK    71

## Scary Stories    75

Telling Terrifying Tales    77
   THE DARK, DARK HOUSE    78
   THE COFFIN    79

## Jokes as Stories    81

Humor as a Starting Point    83
   THE BIG-MOUTH FROG    83

## Family Stories    87

Tales from Your Own Childhood    89
Stories About Your Family    90
   GRANDPA AND THE BLACKSNAKE    90
Folklore from Your Family    93
   THE RAT IN THE CREAM JAR    94

## Stories You Create    97

Stories About Your Child    99
Tales from Your Own Imagination    101
Tales from Your Child's Imagination    103

## More Tales and Tellers    105

## Books to Take You Further    107

## Tale Notes and Sources    111

## Index    115

# Why Tell Stories?

## Introduction

Here is a quick and easy guide to storytelling for parents and grandparents. Nineteen easy-to-tell stories are included to get you started, and I provide lists of more good story sources to help you carry on from here.

Through the centuries storytelling has been an essential part of family life. The intimacy of telling stories enables parents to convey their cultural values. Wrapped in a story, many ideas can be taught, talked about, and tried out. Certain stories serve a family so well that they become an important part of the family's lore.

I hope the short tales included here will start you on this storytelling path. Once you have begun to feel comfortable with the simple act of telling a story, you will find the stories that need to be told in your family will come to you. Some will be stories you read in books or hear from other tellers. Some will be family stories, treasured tales that make up your own unique history. I suggest you start a list right now of "stories we love to share." Add to it as your family discovers and creates its own story trail.

## Why Tell Stories?

Once you have begun telling stories, the sheer joy of the act is all you will need to move you to tell again and again. For those who need a good reason to *start*, here are some of the benefits of storytelling:

**Passing On Values**. All societies use storytelling to instruct their young and to gently admonish each other. Storytelling is a way of "saying without saying." When Anansi the Spider acts in a greedy manner and gets himself into trouble, we all laugh. But a point is taken by the listeners: Being a glutton is *not* acceptable behavior. Watch for stories that speak to the issues you want to confront and add those stories to your list.

**Developing Literary Skills**. In addition to its use in the teaching of values, storytelling makes other educational contributions. Through storytelling the child is exposed to fine language. Children's literary sensibilities are refined and their vocabulary expanded. A sense of story structure is developed, which serves well when the child begins to compose written pieces. And as children begin to join in the telling, their oral skills are developed.

**Recording History**. By telling the stories of our personal, family, and community histories, we are able to make sense of our own past. The things that stick in family memory are the incidents that have been made into stories. To help your child develop a strong sense of family and community, tell and retell their stories.

**Emotional Development**. Storytelling can also play a useful part in the emotional development of your child. Through stories such as folktales the child can encounter danger, overcome obstacles, and share adventures . . . all at a safe distance. The tale's hero or heroine experiences all this *for* the child. Psychologists suggest that such stories help children gain confidence in their *own* ability to handle frightening and difficult situations. The stories provide role models for encountering and overcoming adversity.

**Stretching the Imagination**. There is nothing like a story to stretch the imagination. When you use words alone to weave images, the child soon learns the way into the rich world of the mind. Add stories to your repertoire to take your child to even further realms, and spend time letting your child share his or her own imaginings with you.

**Intimacy**. Last, but perhaps most important, is the intimacy that grows from the story moment. There is a special magic in the sharing of a story with your child. The child cuddles close, you both look away into your imaginations, and the story begins: "Once upon a time . . ." This is a gift you give your child, a gift of time, energy, and caring. The story can be an elaborate fantasy spun from your own dreams, it can be a simple folktale remembered from your childhood, or it can be a story found in a book like this. No matter what the source, the gift is the same . . . a gift of shared imaginations. You need no special skills to share stories with your child. You need only a caring heart and the time to tell.

## Take Time to Tell

Storytelling no longer holds a traditional time slot in our busy contemporary lives. The evening gathering around the fireside when storytelling could take place has been replaced by television. If we want story, we must make a place for it. This does not necessarily mean turning off the TV and forcing a return to an earlier era on the household. There are still many spaces where storytelling can fit usefully into our lives. Here are a few:

**During long drives in the car**. A perfect time to weave tales and to allow the kids a chance to tell stories themselves.

**On cranky afternoons**. Audience-participation stories and tales to act out make good energy users for kids.

**While waiting**. A headful of stories can come in handy during those times when the car is stuck in the shop and you and the kids must kill two hours. Or on the night Mom's plane is late and you and the kids have to sit in the airport for an extra hour.

**At naptime**. Storytelling is the perfect quiet introduction to the afternoon nap for young children.

**At bedtime**. The bedtime story and tucking-in ritual survives in many homes. This is a perfect time to begin sharing stories.

**At active time**. Stories can be part of your high-energy family play, too. Audience-participation tales like "Cheese and Crackers" can provide a rousing good time. Such tellings lead easily to dramatic play. After a few tellings the children know the tales themselves and want to act them out.

**During group sharing**. As your storytelling confidence grows, you may want to share stories with your extended family and with neighborhood children. Eventually you may want to share with Scout or church groups, or in other settings where children and families come together.

Think over your own lifestyle and note spaces you might fill with storytelling. Establish a storytelling tradition by setting aside fifteen minutes every day for a week to share stories in your home. Then, when your family has formed the story habit, let storytelling sift into its most useful places in your lives.

# How to Tell Stories

## How to Tell a Story

In this chapter are some hints for learning a story. However, you don't really need any instruction at all to begin telling stories. You already tell stories every day. When you arrive late for work, you tell the story of the alarm clock that didn't go off and the car that wouldn't start. When Uncle Ed comes to visit, you recount the story of the time he stole the watermelon and almost got shot by Frank Nusbaum. To tell the stories in this book, you will use these same storytelling techniques you already have.

To begin telling a story from this book, just read through the story a couple of times until you are sure you know what happens in the tale. Then imagine that this story happened just down the street and you saw it all. Now tell about it.

For those who feel the need of more specific instructions, here are some hints to help you learn and tell stories. But remember, there is no wrong way to tell a story. You are the teller. You can tell that tale any way you want!

## Hints for Learning a Story

1. Begin with stories you already know. Try folktales you heard as a child, or family stories you remember well.
2. To learn a new story for retelling, simply read it several times.
3. Make a note of the plot line and retell just that to yourself.
   For example, you might make a mental note of this plot line:
   • Gingerbread Man runs away from old woman and old man.
   • Meets cow, horse, farmers, etc.
   • Comes upon river.
   • Fox tells him to climb onto his tail, rump, shoulders, head, nose.
   • Gingerbread Man is eaten.
   You will retell this in your own words. The pleasure of the telling is in your own elaboration. Don't feel bound by the text you read.
4. Note any important plot devices that you must include in order for the story to

make sense. In "The Gingerbread Man," for example, you must hint at the fox's cunning in coaxing the Gingerbread Man onto his nose. This is usually accomplished simply by using a sly voice rather than by saying, "The fox wanted to eat the Gingerbread Man, so he coaxed him onto his nose."

**5**. Notice the mood changes within your story. "The Gingerbread Man" bounces along happily, then changes mood abruptly when the Gingerbread Man meets the fox.

**6**. Note any key phrases within the story that will be fun to say:

> "Run, run, as fast as you CAN.
> You can't catch ME,
> I'm the GINGERBREAD MAN!"

**7**. Decide on an opening phrase and a closing phrase for your story. This may be as simple as "Once upon a time" and "They lived happily ever after." Or "And that's the story of the Little Red Hen!" It is important to open and close with a flourish. But the flourish may be quite simple. Some parents work out a trademark opening and closing that they use every time they tell. For example, bedtime stories might always end: "And the Little Red Hen said, 'That's the end of my story, and it's time for Jenny to go to bed!'" with the lead character sending the child off to sleep each night.

**8**. Practice is the key to perfecting your storytelling. The more you tell, the easier it becomes. But don't worry if you never turn into a "master storyteller." You are doing this for *fun*. It is another way of sharing with your child. No special skills are needed for this—just a willingness to share.

## Hints for Telling the Story

**Tell the story in your own words**. Don't worry about getting the story "right." There is no right way to tell a story. Folktales have been passed from person to person for thousands of years. Every single teller changes the story to fit. Just tell the story in your own way.

**Eye contact**. When telling stories to a group of children, it helps to make good eye contact with the audience as you tell. But when telling to one or two children, it may be more comfortable to hold them on your lap or by your side. Let your words alone reach them as you all look inward to the story.

**Bounces and fingerplays**. When telling to very small children, you may want to incorporate bounces or other tactile elements into your story. "The Gingerbread

Man," for example, could be told while you hold the child on your lap, bouncing the child when the Gingerbread Man chants and runs.

Begin story play with babies and toddlers through use of simple fingerplay stories. These involve manipulation of the child's hand during the telling.

**Audience participation**. If stories have repetitive elements, children may enjoy chiming in on the refrains: "Run, run, as fast as you can . . ." After two or three repetitions of such a refrain, pause and, with a glance, encourage your listeners to join you.

When the children are full of energy, audience participation works well. At times your listeners may even want to act out the parts while you tell the story. However, when these same stories are used at bedtime, a quieter telling, without the participation, may be more effective.

**Technique**. Voice dynamics, dramatic pauses, good breath control, appropriate gesture, eye contact with the audience . . . all these are matters of concern to the teller sharing a story with a large group. If your telling leads you to perform before a Cub Scout pack or at a family reunion, you may want to consult some of the storytelling guides at the end of this book. But for your own home telling, you need not worry too much about technique. The heart of the story is what counts. If you are willing to take the time to share a story, your child will want to listen.

**For more advice**. For those who want to develop storytelling skills even further, a list of books offering advice on storytelling is found on page 107.

# For the Youngest Listeners

# Favorite Nursery Tales

You might want to start storytelling with stories whose plots are already familiar. Even the phrasing in these stories is so well known that whole sentences will jump off your tongue.

Here are three stories you already know. Read each tale through to refresh your memory, then retell it in your own style.

## THE THREE BEARS

Once upon a time,
in a little house in the woods,
there lived three bears.

There was a Mama Bear.
There was a Papa Bear.
And, of course, there was a Baby Bear.

One day Mama Bear made three bowls of porridge.
She put them on the table,
but when the bears began to eat,
the porridge was TOO HOT.
So the three bears went for a walk while the porridge cooled.

While they were gone, along came a little girl.
Her name was GOLDILOCKS.

First she peeped in the window.
Then she knocked at the door.
And then she went inside.

There were three bowls of porridge on the table!
First she tasted Papa Bear's porridge.
It was TOO HOT.

Then she tasted Mama Bear's porridge.
It was TOO COLD.

Then she tasted Baby Bear's porridge.
It was JUST RIGHT.
So she ate it ALL UP.

Now Goldilocks went to sit down.
First she sat on Papa Bear's chair.
It was TOO HARD.

Then she sat on Mama Bear's chair.
It was TOO SOFT.

Then she sat on Baby Bear's chair.
It was JUST RIGHT.

So she sat until she BROKE IT DOWN!

Then Goldilocks ran upstairs to the bedroom.

First she lay on Papa Bear's bed.
It was TOO HARD.

Then she lay on Mama Bear's bed.
It was TOO SOFT.

Then she lay on Baby Bear's bed.
It was JUST RIGHT.
So she fell asleep.

Soon the three bears came home from their walk.

"SOMEONE HAS BEEN EATING MY PORRIDGE!" said Papa Bear.

"Someone has been eating MY PORRIDGE TOO!" said Mama Bear.

"Someone has been eating MY porridge!" said Baby Bear.
"AND THEY ATE IT ALL UP!"
And he began to cry.

Then the three bears went to sit down.

"SOMEONE HAS BEEN SITTING ON MY CHAIR!" said Papa Bear.

"Someone has been sitting on MY CHAIR TOO!" said Mama Bear.

"Someone has been sitting on MY chair!" said Baby Bear.
"AND THEY BROKE IT ALL DOWN!"
And he started to cry again.

Then the three bears went upstairs to the bedroom.

"SOMEONE HAS BEEN SLEEPING ON MY BED!" said Papa Bear.

"Someone has been sleeping on MY BED TOO!" said Mama Bear.

"Someone has been sleeping on MY bed . . ." said Baby Bear,
"and THERE SHE IS!"

At that, Goldilocks woke up!

When she saw the three bears, she was so frightened that she ran out of the house and away into the woods. And the three bears never saw her again.

The end.

**When Telling "The Three Bears."** Most parents have heard this story so many times that they already know its dialogue. This tale can be told quietly if you like, or it can be a good place to try out your *vocal expression*. For those who like histrionics, the range from Baby Bear to Papa Bear allows plenty of room to experiment.

## THE LITTLE RED HEN

Once there was a cat, a dog, a mouse, and a Little Red Hen.

"Let's plant wheat and make some bread!" said the Little Red Hen.

"Good idea!" said the cat.
"Good idea!" said the dog.
"Good idea!" said the mouse.

"Who'll plant the wheat?" asked the Little Red Hen.
"Not I," said the cat.
"Not I," said the dog.
"Not I," said the mouse.
"Then I'll do it myself," said the Little Red Hen.
And she did.

When the wheat was ripe, the cat, the dog, the mouse, and the Little Red Hen went to the field.

"Who'll harvest the wheat?" asked the Little Red Hen.

"Not I," said the cat.

"Not I," said the dog.

"Not I," said the mouse.

"Then I'll do it myself," said the Little Red Hen.

And she did.

> (*This story is very simple. Follow the same pattern to tell the rest of the story.*)

"Who'll thresh the wheat?" asked the Little Red Hen.

"Not I . . ."

"Who'll grind the wheat?" . . .

"Who'll make the bread?" . . .

> (*End the story with:*)

"Who'll eat the bread?" asked the Little Red Hen.

"I will," said the cat.

"I will," said the dog.

"I will," said the mouse.

"No, you won't!" said the Little Red Hen.

"I can do it myself."

And she did.

**When Telling "The Little Red Hen."** Stories like this are easy to learn and easy to tell because the dialogue simply repeats itself over and over. The Little Red Hen and her comrades carry on the same conversation at each step of the story. This type of story pleases *because* of this *repeated dialogue*, so make sure that you stick to the same form each time.

## THE GINGERBREAD MAN

There once was a Little Old Woman and a Little Old Man who were hungry for gingerbread. The Little Old Woman mixed up her dough, rolled it out, and made a nice little gingerbread man. Then she popped that gingerbread man into the oven and waited for it to bake.

But when the baking was done,
the oven door flew open
and out jumped the gingerbread man!
He ran right out the door, calling,

> "Run, run, as fast as you can.
> You can't catch me,
> I'm the gingerbread man!"

The Little Old Woman and the Little Old Man ran out the door after him, calling,

> "Stop, stop, little Gingerbread Man!"

But the Gingerbread Man ran on down the road, calling,

> "Run, run, as fast as you can.
> You can't catch me,
> I'm the gingerbread man!"

Soon he passed a cow.

> "Stop, stop, little Gingerbread Man!" said the cow.

But the Gingerbread Man answered back,

**20**

"I've run away from a Little Old Woman
and a Little Old Man,
And I can run away from YOU, I can.
Run, run, as fast as you CAN.
You can't catch ME,
I'm the GINGERBREAD MAN!"

The Gingerbread Man ran on down the road.
Soon he passed a horse.

*(The story now repeats itself. Each animal or person met calls,
"Stop, stop, little Gingerbread Man!" And the Gingerbread
Man taunts everyone he meets with the same chant. He usually
meets a cow, a horse, a field full of reapers, and a barn full of
threshers. Adapt this to suit yourself. He could meet a field full
of farmers, or even a troop of hiking Cub Scouts. Use the same
dialogue for each.)*

*THE ENDING:*

Then the Gingerbread Man met a FOX.
"Stop, stop, little Gingerbread Man!" said the fox.

"I've run away from a Little Old Woman,
a Little Old Man,
a cow, a horse,
a field full of reapers, a barn full of threshers . . .
and I can run away from YOU, I can.
Run, run, as fast as you CAN.
You can't catch ME,
I'm the GINGERBREAD MAN!"

"Oh, but I wouldn't WANT to catch you," said the fox.
"But I could help you across the river.

Just hop onto my tail,
and I will take you across."

Now the Gingerbread Man had come to a river
and had no other way across.
So the Gingerbread Man hopped onto the fox's tail.
And the fox began to swim the river.

After a while the fox's tail began to droop.
"Hop onto my rump, little Gingerbread Man,
and you will be dry," said the fox.
So the Gingerbread Man hopped onto the fox's rump.

"Hop onto my shoulders, little Gingerbread Man,
and you will keep drier," said the fox.

So the Gingerbread Man hopped onto the fox's shoulders.

"Hop onto my head, little Gingerbread Man,
and you will be drier," said the fox.

So the Gingerbread Man hopped onto the fox's head.

"Hop onto my nose, little Gingerbread Man,
and you will be driest of all," said the fox.
So the Gingerbread Man hopped onto the fox's nose.

Then SNIP, SNAP, the Gingerbread Man
went right down into the fox's tummy.
For that is the way of every Gingerbread Man that ever was made.
Into someone's tummy they go!

**When Telling "The Gingerbread Man."** As in "The Little Red Hen," the dialogue in this story is repeated over and over again. Once you have learned the first sequence, the rest is simply repetition. Notice that this story could be expanded indefinitely by adding more animals or people for the Gingerbread Man to meet on his way. These repeated encounters give the story an easy framework to follow and allow the teller to progress through the story without fear of getting lost.

It is fun to let the audience join in on your refrains in this story:

"Run, run, as fast as you CAN.
You can't catch ME,
I'm the GINGERBREAD MAN!"

This is especially useful when you are telling to lively children who relish the involvement. For quiet times you might want to tell the same story without inviting the audience to participate.

---

Other nursery tales you probably already know include:

"Little Red Riding Hood"
"The Three Little Pigs"
"Henny Penny"
"Three Billy Goats Gruff"

*For more nursery tales see the suggested reading list on page 107.*

---

# Fingerplay Stories

Simple fingerplay stories are often the first tales we share with very young children. The child may be held on your lap as you tell. Here are two fingerplay stories, a handplay story, and a folktale that incorporates fingerplay.

For books containing other fingerplays see the list on page 108.

## THE BEEHIVE

| | |
|---|---|
| Here is the beehive. | *(Show a closed fist.)* |
| Where are the bees? | *(Look the fist over.)* |
| Hidden away where nobody sees. | *(Turn fist slowly and show to audience.)* |
| Soon they'll come creeping out of their hive. | *(Hold fist still.)* |
| One, two, three, four, FIVE! | *(Raise thumb and each finger in quick succession as you count.)* |
| BZZZZZZZ . . . ZZT! | *(Close fist with thumb extended Let your bee-thumb buzz around and "Zzt!" someone!)* |

## FOXIE'S HOLE

| | |
|---|---|
| This is Foxie's hole. | *(Make hole with left hand by closing thumb and forefinger.)* |
| Foxie's not at home. | *(Look inside and show that it is empty.)* |
| Put your finger in. | *(Ask child to put finger into your hand.)* |
| He's gnawing on a bone! | *(Squeeze the child's finger in your hand.)* |

# THE PARROT WITH THE KEY TO ROME

This Chilean tale can be told as a handplay story. It is an endless tale, repeating over and over until the teller laughs, admits the ruse, and stops.

Here's the key to Rome. *(Hold out the pretend key.)*

In Rome there is a street. *(Make snaking motion with hand showing direction of road.)*

In the street there is a house. *(Peak fingers together to form house.)*

In the house there is a room. *(Form square corners with two hands to show room.)*

In the room there is a table. *(Right hand flat as table; left hand perpendicular underneath as table leg.)*

On the table there is a cloth. *(Move left hand to top of right and spread flat as cloth.)*

On the cloth there is a cage. *(Form cage with both hands together.)*

In the cage there is a parrot. *(One hand above the other, palms together, make a parrot beak opening and closing as it talks.)*

And the parrot is saying . . .
Here's the key to Rome.
In Rome there is a street.
*(Etc.)*

Here is the Spanish original as told in Chile:

Esta es la llave de Roma.
Y toma:
En Roma hay una calle,
en la calle una casa,
en la casa un zaguán,
en el zaguán una cocina,
en la cocina una sala,
en la sala una alcoba,
en la alcoba una cama,

**25**

en la cama una dama,
junto a la cama una mesa,
en la mesa una silla,
en la silla una jaula,
en la jaula un parajito,
que dice:
Esta es la llave de Roma.
Y toma . . .

## THE LOST MITTEN

A Russian folktale

This story was probably used as a lap story, told by a grandmother to a child nestled on her lap. The adult makes the mitten and various animals, using hands and fingers to demonstrate their actions.

A little boy was going through the woods to his grandmother's house one sunny winter day.
He had taken off his mittens and stuffed them in his pockets.
As he walked . . . one mitten fell to the ground.
The little boy went on, not knowing he had lost a mitten.

That mitten lay there in the forest.
A brightly colored mitten . . . all by itself.

*(Make a round little cave of your left hand by touching your thumb to your fingertips and curving the hand. This is the mitten. Show it to your listeners.)*

Along came Little-Mouse-Creep-Along.
He ran all around the mitten and had a good look.

**26**

*(The thumb of your right hand is Little-Mouse-Creep-Along. Make him approach and look all around the mitten. Wiggle your thumb when he talks.)*

"What a lovely warm HOUSE for a MOUSE!
I wonder if anyone lives here?"

He began to call:

"Who lives in the mitten?
Who lives in the mitten?
Who lives in the mitten?"

No one answered.
So Little-Mouse-Creep-Along moved right in, bag and baggage,
and set up housekeeping.

*(Put your right thumb into the hole made by thumb and forefinger on your left hand. Keep it there as the other animals arrive.)*

Along came Frog-Croak-a-Lot—

"Gadunk . . . gadunk . . . gadunk . . ."

*(Your right index finger hops up and down as frog approaches "gadunking." Move your index finger as he speaks.)*

"What a fine house for a FROG!
I wonder who lives in the mitten?"

And he began to call:

"Who lives in the mitten?
Who lives in the mitten?

**27**

Who lives in the mitten?"

*(Encourage your listeners to join you in calling "Who lives in the mitten?" This will repeat for each animal in the story.)*

"Little-Mouse-Creep-Along . . . THAT'S WHO!"
*(Move thumb in mitten as mouse replies.)*

"Can I come in too?" *(Move frog finger as it talks.)*

"If there's room for ME,
there's room for YOU.
You can come in too." *(Mouse wiggling again.)*

So Frog-Croak-a-Lot moved right in.
*(Tuck index finger into left hand along with mouse.)*

Along came Hare-Hop-in-the-Hill.
Hop . . . hop . . . hop . . .

*(Raise middle finger of right hand and hop it along. Wiggle the middle finger as hare speaks.)*

"What a house for a HARE!
I wonder who lives in this house?"

"Who lives in the mitten?
Who lives in the mitten?
Who lives in the mitten?" *(Children call with you.)*

"Little-Mouse-Creep-Along!" *(Wiggle mouse thumb inside mitten.)*
"Frog-Croak-a-Lot!" *(Wiggle index finger inside mitten.)*

"Can I come in too?" *(Wiggle middle-finger hare.)*

"If there's room for US,
there's room for YOU.
You can come in TOO." *(Wiggling mouse and frog.)*

So Hare-Hop-in-the-Hill came in.
*(Tuck middle finger into mitten.)*

Next, along came Fox-Run-Everywhere
and Wolf-Leap-out-of-the-Bushes.

*(Wiggle remaining two fingers of right hand. Unless you are un-
usually dextrous, you will not be able to separate these and let
fox and wolf arrive separately. So just bring them in together.)*

"What a fine house for a FOX and a WOLF!
Who could live here?"

"Who lives in the mitten?
Who lives in the mitten?
Who lives in the mitten? *(Children call with you.)*

"Little-Mouse-Creep-Along!" *(Wiggle mouse.)*
"Frog-Croak-a-Lot!" *(Wiggle frog.)*
"Hare-Hop-in-the-Hill!" *(Wiggle hare.)*

"Can we come in too?" *(Wiggle fox and wolf.)*

"If there's room for US,
there's room for YOU.
You can come in TOO!" *(Wiggle mouse, frog, hare.)*

So in came Fox-Run-Everywhere
and Wolf-Leap-out-of-the-Bushes.
*(Tuck remaining two fingers of right hand into mitten.)*

The animals were having a wonderful time.
They were singing and dancing and having a PARTY.
*(Make the mitten and its animals jump around happily.)*

Let's move them over here with their party.
*(Slip fingers of right hand out of mitten and hide them behind your back
as you move the mitten over to the left, still held in front of you but no
longer front center.)*

Because just then, along came BIG-BEAR-SQUASH-THE-WHOLE-LOT-
OF-THEM!
*(Bring right hand out as a fist and stomp it toward the mitten.)*

"What a fine house for a BEAR!
I wonder who lives in this mitten?"

> "WHO LIVES IN THE MITTEN?
> WHO LIVES IN THE MITTEN?
> WHO LIVES IN THE MITTEN?"
> *(Loud and gruffly, shaking fist up and down.)*

"Little-Mouse-Creep-Along!"
*(By this time your audience is probably repeating these lines with you.)*
"Frog-Croak-a-Lot!"
"Hare-Hop-in-the-Hill!"
"Fox-Run-Everywhere!"
"And Wolf-Leap-out-of-the-Bushes!"
"Can *I* come in too?"

> "If there's room for US,
> there's room for YOU.
> You can come in TOO!"

So Big-Bear-Squash-the-Whole-Lot-of-Them
came right in . . .
sat down on the mitten . . .
and SQUASHED-THE-WHOLE-LOT-OF-THEM!
*(Bring right fist over top of mitten, lower it slowly while opening it, and squash mitten hand, opening left hand flat as it gets squashed.)*

**When Telling "The Lost Mitten."** If you are telling this to one or two children, teach them to make the mitten and animals with their own hands. Then when Big-Bear-Squash-the-Whole-Lot-of-Them squashes the mitten, *you* become the bear and squash *their* little mitten hands.

**About "The Lost Mitten."** Versions of this tale have been collected from several Russian tellers. The animals mentioned change, but the story always ends with the destruction of the "house." You might like to read the Ukranian version in the picture book *The Mitten,* by Jan Brett (New York: Putnam, 1989), with your children and talk about the differences between that version and this story.

# Bedtime Stories, Expandable Tales, and Endless Tales

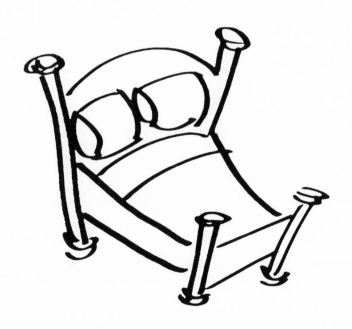

# Bedtime Stories

Bedtime is often a favorite time for story sharing. Children are in a quieter mood, or you would like them to be so. Quiet tales and repetitive tales that drone on a bit are useful at this time of day. Expandable tales and endless tales come in handy here. These enable the storyteller to keep telling until the child falls asleep.

A grandmother from the Marshall Islands told of her favorite bedtime story. Sea birds and sea creatures arrived one by one at an island. She just kept bringing in more birds and more sea creatures until every child was asleep. "The next night they would ask how the story had *ended*, and I would start all over again!"

Another type of story that families enjoy at day's end is a tale *about* your child. This is a way to revisit the events of the day, helping your child sort things out and remember. See "Stories About Your Child," page 99, for more on this.

Here is an enjoyable bedtime tale that deals with childhood fears of being left alone in the dark. I heard this story from Elizabeth Miller, a New Zealand teller.

## THE SQUEAKY DOOR

There once was a little boy
who went to his granny's house for a visit.
Granny said, "I have a surprise for you tonight!
You are going to sleep in the BIG BRASS BED!
You get to sleep in the guest bedroom . . . all by yourself!"

When bedtime came, she took the little boy upstairs
and tucked him into the BIG BRASS BED.

She kissed the little boy good night—SMACK.
She said, "Now when I turn off the light and close the door,

are you going to be frightened?"
And the little boy said, "NO, not ME."

So Granny went out and turned off the light—CLICK.
And she clo-o-o-sed the door—SQUE-E-E-E.
Oh! What a scary sound!
The little boy began to CRY!—"Boo-hoo-hoo-hoo . . ."

Granny ran back into the room.
"Oh my goodness! Were you frightened?"
"No . . . not me." (In a very tiny voice.)
"Well, I know what would make you feel more comfortable.
How would you like to have the CAT sleep with you?"
"Oh, YES! I'd LIKE that."
So Granny went downstairs and got the cat out of the cat basket.

She brought the cat upstairs.
She tucked the cat in.
She tucked the little boy in.
She kissed the boy good night—SMACK.
She kissed the cat good night—SMACK.
She said, "Now. When I turn off the light and close the door,
are you going to be frightened?"
And little boy said, "NO. Not ME!"

So Granny turned off the light—CLICK.
And she clo-o-o-sed the door—SQUE-E-E-E.

The cat began to MEOW!
"Meow! Meow! Meow!"
The little boy began to CRY!
"Boo-hoo-hoo . . ."

Granny ran back into the room.
"Oh my goodness! Were you frightened?"

"No . . . not me."
"Let me see . . .
How would you like to have the DOG sleep with you?"
"Oh, YES! I'd LIKE that."
So Granny went downstairs and got the dog out of the doghouse.

She brought the dog upstairs.
She tucked the dog in.
She tucked the cat in.
She tucked the little boy in.
She kissed the little boy good night—SMACK.
She kissed the cat good night—SMACK.
She kissed the dog good night—SMACK.
She said, "Now. When I turn off the light and close the door,
are you going to be frightened?"
And Little Boy said, "NO. Not ME!"

So Granny turned off the light—CLICK.
and she clo-o-o-sed the door—SQUE-E-E-E.

The dog began to BARK!
"Woof! Woof! Woof!"
The cat began to MEOW!
"Meow! Meow! Meow!"
The little boy began to CRY!
"Boo-hoo-hoo . . ."

Granny ran back into the room.
"Oh my goodness! Were you frightened?"
"No . . . not me."
"Let me see . . .
How would you like to have the PIGGY sleep with you?"
"Oh, YES! I'd LIKE that."

So Granny went out to the pigpen and got the pig.

She brought the pig upstairs.
She tucked the pig in.
She tucked the dog in.
She tucked the cat in.
She tucked the little boy in.
She kissed the little boy good night—SMACK.
She kissed the cat good night—SMACK.
She kissed the dog good night—SMACK.
She kissed the pig good night—(*Hold your nose and . . .* )
   SMACK.
She said, "Now. When I turn off the light and close the door,
are you going to be frightened?"
And Little Boy said, "NO. Not ME!"

So Granny turned off the light—CLICK.
and she clo-o-o-sed the door—SQUE-E-E-E.

The pig began to GRUNT!
"Grunt! Grunt! Grunt!"
The dog began to BARK!
"Woof! Woof! Woof!"
The cat began to MEOW!
"Meow! Meow! Meow!"
The little boy began to CRY!
"Boo-hoo-hoo . . ."

Granny ran back into the room.
"Oh my goodness! Were you frightened?"
"No . . . not me."
"Let me see . . .
How would you like to have the HORSIE to sleep with you?"
"Oh, YES! I'd LIKE that!"

So Granny went out to the stable and got the horse.

She led the horse up the stairs. She tucked the horse in.
She tucked the pig in.
She tucked the dog in.
She tucked the cat in.
She tucked the little boy in.
She kissed the little boy good night—SMACK.
She kissed the cat good night—SMACK.
She kissed the dog good night—SMACK.
She kissed the pig good night—SMACK.
She kissed the horse good night—SMACK.
She said, "Now. When I turn off the light and close the door,
are you going to be frightened?"
And Little Boy said, "NO. Not ME!"

So Granny turned off the light—CLICK.
And she clo-o-o-sed the door—SQUE-E-E-E.

The horse began to NEIGH!
"Neigh! Neigh! Neigh!"
The pig began to GRUNT!
"Grunt! Grunt! Grunt!"
The dog began to BARK!
"Woof! Woof! Woof!"
The cat began to MEOW!
"Meow! Meow! Meow!"
The little boy began to CRY!
"Boo-hoo-hoo . . ."
They all JUMPED UP IN BED and made such a ruckus that . . .
they BROKE the bed!
Down it fell with a CRASH!

Granny came running back into the room.
"Oh my goodness! This will never do!
This will NEVER do!"

Granny led the horse back down the stairs
and put it back in the stable.
Granny carried the pig back down the stairs
and put it back in the pigpen.
She carried the dog back downstairs
and put it back in the doghouse.
She carried the cat back downstairs
and put it back in the cat basket.
Then she carried the little boy over
and put him in bed with her and Grandpa for the night.

The next day Granny got out her toolbox.
She hammered and she nailed,
and she put that bed back together again.
Then she got out her can of oil
and she OILED the hinges on that squeaky door—
    GLUB GLUB GLUB . . . SQUEEEE . . . SQUEEEE . . . SQUEEE . . .
and she OILED the hinges on that squeaky door—
    GLUB GLUB GLUB . . . SQUEE . . . SQUEE . . . SQUEE . . .
    (softer squeak)
and she OILED the hinges on that squeaky door—
    GLUB GLUB GLUB . . . SHHH . . . SHHH . . . SHHH . . .
until the squeak was all gone.

That night she tucked the little boy into the big brass bed.
She put the cat on one side.
And NOBODY else.
Then Granny kissed the little boy good night—SMACK. (soft)
And she kissed the cat good night—SMACK. (softer)
And she said, "Now. When I turn off the light and close the door,
are you going to be frightened?"
And little boy said, "No. . . . Not me. . . ."

So Granny tiptoed out and turned off the light—CLICK.

**40**

And she clo-o-osed the door—SHHHH . . .
And she listened.
And she heard the little boy . . .
"Shnnn . . . shnnn . . . shnnn . . ." *(Snoring)*
And she listened.
And she heard the cat . . .
"Zznnn . . . zznnn . . . zznnn . . ."

And that's the story of the Granny, and the little boy,
and the squeaky door.

**When Telling "The Squeaky Door."**   It is fun to add sound effects to the grandmother's exit from the bedroom. "She kissed him good night—SMACK." Make a big kissing sound. "She turned off the light—CLICK." Make this sound by clicking your tongue. And of course make the door's SQUE-E-E-E very dramatic.

After hearing the first episode, your children will want to say the little boy's line with you. "Are you going to be frightened when I close the door?" you ask. And the children join in as the little boy replies, "No. . . . Not  me. . . ."

Most tellers will want to bark, meow, grunt, and neigh with the animals. And your listeners may want to join in, too.

# Expandable Stories

Some stories allow a natural extension by the teller. When you are telling "The Squeaky Door," for example, it is easy to add in animals. Your audience may want to suggest animals to add and tell you just what racket each made. This kind of expandable story is useful when you have a lot of time to fill, or when you are trying to satisfy a seemingly limitless demand for storytelling from your listeners. In some cultures this is a popular way to end a story session at bedtime. The teller just keeps the story going until everyone drops off to sleep!

Here is a short tale from the Chucha people of Siberia, "Ms. Mouse Needs a Friend." This could be expanded to great length by letting your listeners suggest more animal rescuers for Ms. Mouse.

## MS. MOUSE NEEDS A FRIEND

One cold winter morning Ms. Mouse woke up feeling thirsty.
She found her little cup and her little hatchet
and went right down to the frozen pond.
Ms. Mouse sat down and went to work.
First she chopped a hole in the ice.
Then she dipped her cup in the cool water and began to drink.
"Aaahhh." How good that cold water tasted!
Ms. Mouse drank it all down.
She dipped her little cup and had another cool drink.
"Aaaahhh." Just one more.
Ms. Mouse dipped her cup and drank again.

Ms. Mouse packed away her cup and started to stand up.
But, "Oh! Oh!"
Ms. Mouse had sat still on the ice so long,
her TAIL had frozen fast to the ice!

> "Eee! Eee!
> I'm STUCK!
> Eee! Eee!
> I'm STUCK!"

She began to wail.

Then Ms. Mouse thought, "I must find a friend to rescue me.
Who could I call on for help?"
She remembered Snowshoe Rabbit.
Ms. Mouse began to call,

> "Snowshoe Rabbit!
> Help, help!
> Snowshoe Rabbit!
> Help, help!
> I need a friend!"

Snowshoe Rabbit heard her.
He came out of his hole and
looked around.
"Ms. Mouse must be in trouble!"
Snowshoe Rabbit leaped down the hillside to help her.
"Don't worry, Ms. Mouse.
I'll be your friend."
Snowshoe Rabbit reached out his paw to help her.

But when she saw him coming, Ms. Mouse began to snicker.
"Oh, look at those BIG FEET.
What STUPID BIG FEET Snowshoe Rabbit has!"

When Snowshoe Rabbit heard her, he stopped.
His feelings were hurt.
"I guess she doesn't want me for a friend after all."
Snowshoe Rabbit turned around and went back to his hole.

Ms. Mouse was still stuck on the ice.
"Oh, oh," said Ms. Mouse.
"Maybe I said the wrong thing."
She began to struggle again.

    "Eee! Eee!
    I'm STUCK!
    Eee! Eee!
    I'm STUCK!"

Who could she call?
Maybe Mink could help.

    "Mink!
    Help, help!
    Mink!
    Help, help!
    I need a friend!"

Mink heard Ms. Mouse calling.
He came out of his den.
"I'm coming, Ms. Mouse.
I'll be your friend."
Mink came racing down the path to the pond.
He put out his paw to help Ms. Mouse.

But when Mink came close, Ms. Mouse began to snicker.
"Yuck, yuck, what BAD BREATH you have!
*Ick*, what BAD BREATH!"

Mink was offended.
"Maybe she doesn't want me for a friend after all."
Mink turned away and scurried back to his den.

"Oh, oh," said Ms. Mouse.
"Maybe I said the wrong thing."
And she began to wail again.

> "Eee! Eee!
> I'm STUCK!
> Eee! Eee!
> I'm STUCK!"

Who could she call?
Fox! He might help.

> "Fox!
> Help, help!
> Fox!
> Help, help!
> I need a friend!"

Fox, sleeping in his den, heard her.
"I'm coming, Ms. Mouse.
I'll be your friend."
And Fox came running to help.
But before he could put out his paw to aid her,
Ms. Mouse began to snicker.
"Just look at that LONG TAIL!
What an UGLY TAIL!"
Fox felt very bad.
"Maybe she doesn't want me for a friend after all."
Fox turned and hurried back to his home.

"Oh, oh," said Ms. Mouse.
"Maybe I said the wrong thing."
She was still stuck.

> "Eee! Eee!
> I'm STUCK!
> Eee! Eee!
> I'm STUCK!"

Who could she call?
Bear!

> "Bear!
> Help, help!
> Bear!
> Help, help!
> I need a friend!"

Bear was sleeping in his den.
He heard that mouse calling and calling.
Bear jumped up.
Bear lunged out of his den.
He gallumphed right down to the frozen pond . . .
  *WHACK!*
With one stroke of his huge paw, he knocked Ms. Mouse free.
Then he was gone back up the hill and into his den before she
could say one thing.
Ms. Mouse was free.
But that huge bear had hit her so hard that it had broken her
little tail right off.
Poor Ms. Mouse.
She ran off to her little home crying,

"Eee! Eee!
I chose the wrong friend!
Eee! Eee!
I chose the wrong friend!"

Don't be like Ms. Mouse.
If someone offers you a hand in friendship, take it.
Just overlook any faults and be a friend.
Or you might end up like Ms. Mouse . . .
with a strong friend, but NO TAIL!

**When Telling "Ms. Mouse Needs a Friend."** You may use this retelling as an outline for your own first telling. When you tell the tale again, let your listeners suggest animals Ms. Mouse might call on for help. They can also tell you which faults she found with each animal. The pattern can be repeated indefinitely to suit your tastes.

After hearing the story once, your children will probably want to join you on Ms. Mouse's cries of "Eee! Eee! I'm STUCK!" After a few tellings they will likely be telling most of the story *with* you. They may even want to act the story out.

The moral ending to the story is optional. A story can always be left to makes its point without an obvious statement of the moral.

# Endless Tales: The Storyteller's Exit

Sometimes tellers tire of telling before their audiences tire of listening. Especially at bedtime you may find your children developing an insatiable thirst for "just one more story." For centuries storytellers have been solving this problem with a trick: the endless tale. The teller innocently starts a story, but the listeners soon realize the trick and call a halt to the storytelling.

Here are three endless tales. See page 25 for yet another.

## A DARK AND STORMY NIGHT

It was a dark and stormy night.
The captain stood on the bridge and said to the mate,
"Tell me a story."
So the mate began:
"It was a dark and stormy night.
The captain stood on the bridge and said to the mate,
'Tell me a story.'
So the mate began:
'It was a dark and stormy night . . .' "

## A SILLY QUESTION

Once there was a girl who asked her father,
"What's a silly question?"
And her father replied:
"Once there was a girl who asked her father,
'What's a silly question?'
And her father replied:
'Once . . .' "

## THE BIRD CATCHER

Once a bird catcher discovered his net FULL of birds.
There must have been HUNDREDS of birds caught in his net.
The bird catcher was delighted.
But right before his eyes, a parrot caught within
pecked a hole through the net and flew out.
Flippity—flippity—flippity—flip . . .
The bird catcher dropped his net and ran after that parrot.

But just then ANOTHER bird escaped through the hole.
Flippity—flippity—flippity—flip . . .
So the bird catcher ran after THAT bird.

And then ANOTHER bird escaped . . .
Flippity—flippity—flippity—flip . . .

*(Keep this up until your audience complains. Tell them that all
the birds must escape before the story can continue. When they
groan, put them to bed.)*

# Easy-to-Tell Folktales

# Participation Folktales

Folktales are often easy to retell. They have been passed on for hundreds of years by word of mouth. So you are just one more teller in the chain. And like every teller who ever told these tales, you will change them to suit yourself and your child.

Many folktales offer a chance for listeners to chime in by chanting, singing, or joining the teller in repeated phrases. These are fun for your rowdier moments of storytelling. If you find yourself telling to large groups of children, these audience-participation tales are especially useful.

To tell these audience-participation stories effectively, simply give your audience an encouraging glance and a nod when you want them to join in a refrain. If they seem reticent, ask, "Do you want to help me say it?" Of course, at quiet moments like bedtime it is best to tell them *without* the rousing participation.

Here is one of my favorite participation stories. It is an Appalachian tale, but feel free to adapt the language to fit your own speech patterns.

## CHEESE AND CRACKERS

One time there was an Old Woman, an Old Man, a Little Girl,
a Little Boy, and a pet Squirrel.
Those folks had a little baby that never would hush up.
One day that baby woke up,
and it was bawling for cheese and crackers:

"Cheese and crackers!
Cheese and crackers!
I've gotta have some
Cheese and crackers!"

The Old Woman said, "LAWS! That baby won't hush up.
Little Boy, run down to the store
and buy that baby a nickel's worth of cheese and crackers."
So Little Boy took the nickel and ran out of the house.
He was happy to be going to the store.
Started singing:

"Cheese and crackers!
Cheese and crackers!
I'm gonna buy some
Cheese and crackers!"

Didn't look where he was going and . . .
                    KA-WHUMP!
He bumped right into a big Old Bear sleeping on the path.
Little Boy jumped back.
Said, "MY, you're a FAT OLD BEAR!"
Old Bear rose up.

"I may be FAT.
But I'm gonna be FATTER!
'Cause I'm gonna EAT YOU UP!"

Little Boy said,
"No you WON'T.
'Cause I can RUN!"
Old Bear said,
"You can RUN.
But I can JUMP!"

**54**

And that Old Bear jumped and—Glump! Glump!—
he swallowed that Little Boy down.
Him and his nickel, too.

Meanwhile back home the baby had not stopped crying:

> "Cheese and crackers!
> Cheese and crackers!
> I've gotta have some
> Cheese and crackers!"

Old Woman said, "LAWS! That baby won't hush up.
Little Girl, run down to the store
and buy that baby a nickel's worth of cheese and crackers."
Little Girl took the nickel and ran out of the house.
Ran down the road singing:

> "Cheese and crackers!
> Cheese and crackers!
> I'm gonna buy some
> Cheese and crackers!"

Didn't look where she was going and . . .
> KA-WHUMP!
She bumped right into that big Old Bear.
Little Girl jumped back.
Said, "MY, you're a FAT OLD BEAR!"
Old Bear rose up.

> "I may be FAT.
> But I'm gonna be FATTER!
> 'Cause I'm gonna EAT YOU UP!"

"No you WON'T.
'Cause I can RUN," said the Little Girl.
"You can RUN.
But I can JUMP!"
And that Old Bear jumped and—Glump! Glump!—
he swallowed that Little Girl down.
Her and her nickel, too.

Back home the baby was still bawling:

> "Cheese and crackers!
> Cheese and crackers!
> I've gotta have some
> Cheese and crackers!"

"LAWS!" said the Old Woman. "That baby won't hush up.
Old Man, would you go down to the store
and buy that baby some cheese and crackers?"
So the Old Man took a nickel and off he went.
He was happy to be out of the house!

> "Cheese and crackers!
> Cheese and crackers!
> I'm gonna buy some
> Cheese and crackers!"

Didn't look where he was going, and
            KA-WHUMP!
He bumped right into that big Old Bear.
Old Man stepped back.
"MY, you're a FAT OLD BEAR!"
Old Bear rose up.

> "I may be FAT.
> But I'm gonna be FATTER!
> 'Cause I'm gonna eat you up!"

"Oh no you WON'T," said the Old Man.
" 'Cause I can RUN!"
"Well YOU can RUN.
But I can JUMP!"
And the Old Bear jumped and—Glump! Glump!—
he swallowed that Old Man down.
Him and his nickel, too.

Meanwhile back home that baby was STILL crying!

"Cheese and crackers!
Cheese and crackers!
I've gotta have some
Cheese and crackers!"

Old Woman said "LAWS! That baby won't hush up.
I guess I'd better go to town myself
and get some cheese and crackers."
Said, "Little Squirrel, you watch the baby while I'm gone."
And she ran off down the road.

"Cheese and crackers!
Cheese and crackers!
I'm gonna buy some
Cheese and crackers!"

Well, she didn't look where she was going, and
                    KA-WHUMP!
She bumped smack dab into that big Old Bear,
stood back and said, "MY, you sure are a FAT OLD BEAR!"
Old Bear rose up.

"I may be FAT!
But I'm gonna be FATTER!
'Cause I'm gonna EAT YOU UP!"

"Oh no you WON'T," said Old Woman.
" 'Cause I can RUN!"
"You can RUN.
But I can JUMP!"
And that Old Bear jumped and—Glump! Glump!—
he swallowed her down.
The Old Woman and her nickel, too.

Back home that baby had not hushed up!

"Cheese and crackers!
Cheese and crackers!
I've gotta have some
Cheese and crackers!"

Little Squirrel said, "LAWS! That baby will not hush up!
Guess I'd better go to town myself
and buy it some cheese and crackers."
Little Squirrel took the lid off the sugar bowl
and took out a nickel. He went running down the road.

"Cheese and crackers!
Cheese and crackers!
Buy that baby some
Cheese and crackers!"

Didn't look where he was going, and
KA-WHUMP!
He ran smack dab into that big Old Bear.
Little Squirrel stood back.
Said, "MY, you're a FAT OLD BEAR!"
That Old Bear rose up and started in.

"I may be FAT.
But I'm gonna be FATTER!
'Cause I'm gonna EAT YOU UP!"

Little Squirrel did not say a thing.
He just jumped off the road and ran up a tree, quick as anything.
Said, "You can't eat ME. 'Cause I can run up a tree!"
Old Bear said,
"If a Little Squirrel can run up a tree . . .
a big Old Bear can run up a tree!"
And he started climbing that tree after the squirrel.
Little Squirrel ran clear to the top of that tree.
Called down,
"You can't catch ME.
'Cause I can climb to the tip top of this tree!"
Big Old Bear said,
"If a Little Squirrel can climb to the tip top of this tree . . .
a big Old Bear can climb to the tip top of this tree."
And he started climbing clear to the top of that tree.
Little Squirrel climbed out on a little limb.
"You can't catch ME. 'Cause I can climb out on a little limb!"
Old Bear said,
"If a Little Squirrel can climb out on that little limb . . .
a big Old Bear can climb out on that little limb."
And he climbed right out after him.
Little Squirrel said,
"You can't catch ME.
'Cause I can JUMP to the next TREE!"
And he JUMPED to the next tree.
Old Bear said,
"If a Little Squirrel can jump to the next tree . . .
a big Old Bear can jump to the next tree!"

And that big Old Bear gave one JUMP
    to the
        next
           tree
              but he
                  didn't
                      make it . . .
                              *KA-WHUMP!*

That Old Bear hit the ground.
And when he hit . . .
out popped the Old Woman.
She said, "I'm OUT. And my NICKEL, too!"
Out popped the Old Man.
He said, "I'm OUT. And my NICKEL, too!"
Out popped the Little Girl.
Said, "I'm OUT. And my NICKEL, too!"
Out popped the Little Boy.
Said, "I'm OUT. And my NICKEL, too!"

And Little Squirrel up in the tree looked down and laughed.
Said, "I'm OUT. 'Cause I never was IN!"

Then that Old Bear groaned.
Said,

    "I may have been FAT.
    But I sure am THINNER!"

Those folks counted out their money, and they had five . . .
ten . . . fifteen . . . twenty . . . twenty-five cents in NICKELS!
So they went on down to the store.

    "CHEESE AND CRACKERS!
    CHEESE AND CRACKERS!

WE'RE GONNA BUY SOME
CHEESE AND CRACKERS!"

And they bought TWENTY-FIVE CENTS' worth
of CHEESE AND CRACKERS! Took that home,
and they FED that baby cheese and crackers . . .
and they FED that baby cheese and crackers . . .
and they FED that baby cheese and crackers . . .
until that baby HUSHED UP!

**When Telling "Cheese and Crackers."**  Since this story is a little longer than
the others, you may need some tips for remembering it. Think of the story as a series of
events and moods. In the first part of the story folks keep repeating the same action.
They go down the road chanting, meet the fat old bear, and carry on the same conversation each time. This repetition makes the tale easy to remember. At the story's climax
the mood changes from bouncy repetition to suspense. Little Squirrel climbs the tree . . .
the bear climbs after. Your telling mood will change here for dramatic effect. At the
story's end, return to your bouncy mood again as everyone goes off down the road chanting. Then give the tale's final lines very deliberately: "And they FED that baby cheese
and crackers . . . and they FED that baby cheese and crackers . . . and they FED that baby
cheese and crackers . . . until that baby HUSHED UP!"

I like to make the KA-WHUMP! very dramatic when I tell this. It stops the whole story
for a moment while both teller and bumper catch their breath.

Of course the audience will want to join you on your "Cheese and crackers!" chants.

You may want to use this tune for your "Cheese and crackers!" chant. I made it up,
so any tune or rhythm you want to use would be just as good. Remember that this is a
folktale. It is *okay* to change it and make it feel like your own story.

Cheese and crack-ers!  Cheese and crack-ers!  I'm gonna buy some  Cheese and crack-ers!

# Folktales with Many Variants

As folktales are passed from teller to teller, they move between cultures. Travelers hear good stories and bring them home. Printed books carry stories everywhere. Since every new teller changes the story a little, many variants of a tale come into existence. To find other variants of the stories in this book, check the "Tale Notes and Sources" section starting page 111. And if you enjoy looking at several different versions of one tale, check the books listed on page 108. It can be fun to tell or read several variations of one tale, or even to make up your own!

Here is a story from the Nanai people of eastern Siberia. This tale is told in slightly different ways all over the world. At the end of the tale are notes about other ways in which this tale has been told. You might try retelling the same tale with several different twists.

## STRONGEST ONE OF ALL

Two boys were skating on the Amur River.
Suddenly the two boys collided. WHUMP!
One of the boys fell onto the ice.
The other boy remained standing.
The standing boy began to brag.
"Look at this! He fell, but I still stand!

I must be the Strongest One of All!
You should all bow to ME.
I am STRONGEST ONE OF ALL!"
The other children giggled and began to bow
to the bragging boy.
"Oh, yes. You are . . .

     Strongest One of All
     Strongest One of All!"

They laughed and bowed.
The boy danced about, bragging.
Suddenly he slipped and fell on the ice.
              WHUMP!
He hit his head hard.
The boy sat up rubbing his head
while his fallen friend started to laugh.
"YOU are not the Strongest One of All.
There is someone stronger than YOU.
ICE! Ice just whacked your head!"
"You are right," said the boy.
"Then we should be bowing to . . . ICE!"
The children laughed and began to bow to ICE.

     "Strongest One of All!
     Strongest One of All!"

But Ice looked up and said,
"Stop that, you silly children!
I am not the Strongest One of All.
There is someone much stronger than I.
When SUN comes out, I melt.
SUN is stronger than Ice."

The children looked at one another.
"Then we should be bowing to . . . SUN."
And they began to bow.

> "Strongest One of All.
> Strongest One of All."

Sun looked down from the sky and called,
"Stop that, you foolish children!
I am not the Strongest One of All.
There is someone much stronger than I."

Just then Cloud came along.
Cloud covered Sun's face and Sun disappeared.
The children understood.
"Then CLOUD is the Strongest One of All.
We should be bowing to . . . CLOUD."
And they began to bow.

> "Strongest One of All.
> Strongest One of All."

But Cloud called, "Don't be SILLY.
There is someone much stronger than I.
WIND is stronger than I am."

Wind came along and gave one puff . . .
and Cloud was blown out of sight.
"Then we should be bowing to . . . WIND!"
The children turned and bowed to the wind.

> "Strongest One of All.
> Strongest One of All."

But Wind said, "Stop that silly bowing!
I am not the Strongest One of All.
True, I race over the valleys.
But when I come to the MOUNTAIN,
I am broken to pieces.
Even *I* cannot move the mountain.
Mountain is stronger than Wind."
"Oh, now we see," said the children.
"We should be bowing to . . . MOUNTAIN!"
And they began to bow to the Mountain.

> "Strongest One of All.
> Strongest One of All."

"Foolish children," said Mountain.
"There is someone stronger than I.
The Tree that grows on my shoulder is stronger.
That Tree pushes its roots into my shoulder.
Those roots break apart my rocks,
TREE is stronger than I."
"Then we should be bowing to . . . TREE!"
The children began to bow.

> "Strongest One of All.
> Strongest One of All."

Then Tree said . . .
"That's RIGHT!
Here I AM!
The Strongest One of All!
You can bow to me.
Just go ahead and bow."
And Tree waved its branches proudly.
The children started to bow.

"Strongest One of All.
Strongest One of All . . ."

Then they stopped.
They laughed.
"Our fathers are WOODCUTTERS.
They cut down trees every day.
Tree isn't the Strongest One of All!"

The children ran to get their little hatchets.
They began to chop.
WHACK . . . WHACK . . . WHACK . . . WHACK . . .
CREEEEAAAAKKKK . . . KAPLOMB!
They chopped that tree right down.
Since then the people of the Amur River say,
"MAN is the Strongest One of All."
They may not be right.
But that is what they say.

**When Telling "The Strongest One of All."** I pretend to bow to the boy, Ice, Sun, etc., as I tell this story, bowing rapidly over and over as I repeat "Strongest One of All! Strongest One of All!" The children love to join in this, giggling as they bow.

**Other Versions of This Story.** FROM INDIA: A lady mouse refuses all suitors. She says she wants to marry the strongest one in the world. It turns out that mouse, who gnaws on Mountain, is strongest. So she marries him. (*Usha the Mouse-Maiden*, by Mehli Gobhai [New York: Hawthorn Books, 1969].)

FROM JAPAN: A stone-cutter is unhappy with his lot. He wishes he were strong like the sun. It turns out that the stone-cutter is strongest of all, as he can hew the mountain. (*The Stone-Cutter*, by Gerald McDermott [New York: Viking, 1975].)

FROM KOREA: A mole is to wed sky, sun, cloud, wind, a stone statue, a mole. (*Tales of a Korean Grandmother*, by Frances Carpenter [Garden City, New York: Doubleday, 1947].)

FROM VIETNAM: Cat wants to take the name of the strongest creature. Heaven, cloud, wind, wall, mouse, cat. (*The Toad Is the Emperor's Uncle* by Vo-Dinh [Garden City, New York: Doubleday, 1970].)

# Story Stretches

When children get wiggly, it is time for a *very* active story. Story stretches fill this bill. These are lively bits of story play that get the children on their feet and moving. Storytellers who tell to large groups of children use stories like these, along with action songs, to help children shake their wiggles out.

I learned this story from an uncle at a family reunion when I was growing up in Southern Indiana. He used it to entertain the restless children who were rousting about while their elders sat and talked. You may have heard a version of this in your own childhood. Remember that these folktales are changed by every teller, so they appear in many different forms. For other versions of this story, see page 113. And if you want more story stretches, see the list on page 108.

## LET'S GO ON A BEAR HUNT!

*(Ask your audience to repeat everything you say and make the motions with you.)*

| **Teller:** | **Audience:** |
| --- | --- |
| Let's go on a BEAR HUNT! | Let's go on a BEAR HUNT! |
| All right! | All right! |
| Let's GO! | Let's GO! |

*(Begin slapping legs rhythmically in a one-two-three-four beat. Keep this up until your listeners are all slapping their legs along with you. Keep up the rhythmic leg slapping in time to your words as you repeat the chants.)*

Oh, LOOK!                Oh, LOOK!
There's a BRIDGE!       There's a BRIDGE!
Can't go 'ROUND it.     Can't go 'ROUND it.
Can't go UNDER it.      Can't go UNDER it.
Better go OVER it.      Better go OVER it.
All right!               All right!
Let's GO!              Let's GO!

*(Begin thumping your fists on your chest, making a hollow sound, as you cross the bridge. Once on the other side, begin slapping your legs again.)*

Oh, LOOK!                Oh, LOOK!
There's a SWAMP!      There's a SWAMP!
Can't go 'ROUND it.     Can't go 'ROUND it.
Can't go UNDER it.      Can't go UNDER it.
Better go THROUGH it.   Better go THROUGH it.
All right!               All right!
Let's GO!              Let's GO!

*(Move arms in front of you as if pushing aside weeds as you struggle through the marshy swamp. Make a swishing noise, keeping your rhythm, as you go. All do this in unison.)*

SWISH. SWISH. SWISH. SWISH.    SWISH. SWISH. SWISH. SWISH.

*(Begin slapping your legs again once you have passed through the swamp.)*

Oh, LOOK!                Oh, LOOK!
There's a LAKE!        There's a LAKE!
Can't go 'ROUND it.     Can't go 'ROUND it.
Can't go UNDER it.      Can't go UNDER it.
Better go THROUGH it.   Better go THROUGH it.
All right!               All right!
Let's GO!              Let's GO!

*(All make swimming motions rhythmically in unison until lake is crossed, then revert to leg slapping again.)*

| | |
|---|---|
| Oh, LOOK! | Oh, LOOK! |
| There's a DEEP DARK WOODS! | There's a DEEP DARK WOODS! |
| Can't go 'ROUND it. | Can't go 'ROUND it. |
| Can't go UNDER it. | Can't go UNDER it. |
| Better go THROUGH it. | Better go THROUGH it. |
| All right! | All right! |
| Let's GO! | Let's GO! |

*(Begin pushing branches aside as you walk, and begin talking in more hushed tones.)*

| | |
|---|---|
| Oh, LOOK! | Oh, LOOK! |
| There's a CAVE! | There's a CAVE! |
| Can't go 'ROUND it. | Can't go 'ROUND it. |
| Can't go UNDER it. | Can't go UNDER it. |
| Better go THROUGH it. | Better go THROUGH it. |
| All right! | All right! |
| Let's GO! | Let's GO! |

*(Begin to tiptoe, slapping your leg very gently and very quietly. . . .)*

| | |
|---|---|
| OOOOOHHHHHHH . . . | OOOOOHHHHHHH . . . |
| It's DARK in here. | It's DARK in here. |
| I SMELL something. *(Sniff.)* | I SMELL something. *(Sniff.)* |
| It smells like a bear. | It smells like a bear. |
| I HEAR something. *(Listen.)* | I HEAR something. *(Listen.)* |
| It sounds like a BEAR. | It sounds like a BEAR. |
| I FEEL something. | I FEEL something. |

*(Feel around in front of you.)*

| | |
|---|---|
| It FEELS like a BEAR. | It FEELS like a BEAR. |
| I SEE something. | I SEE something. |

*(Make eyeglasses with hands and peer.)*

It LOOKS like a BEAR.  
It IS a BEAR!  
Let's get OUT OF HERE!

It LOOKS like a BEAR.  
It IS a BEAR!  
Let's get OUT OF HERE!

*(Everything is acted out in reverse as quickly as possible.)*

Out of the CAVE!  
Through the DEEP DARK  
    WOODS!  
Swim the LAKE!  
Through the SWAMP!  
Across the BRIDGE!  
Into my HOUSE!  
And SLAM THE DOOR!

Out of the CAVE!  
Through the DEEP DARK  
    WOODS!  
Swim the LAKE!  
Through the SWAMP!  
Across the BRIDGE!  
Into my HOUSE!  
And SLAM THE DOOR!

*(Stop and relax, wipe your brow in exhaustion.)*

Whew!  
We made it back HOME!

Whew!  
We made it back HOME!

**When Telling "Let's Go on a Bear Hunt."** Set up your rhythm for leg slapping and keep it going throughout the story. Your swimming motions, climbing motions, etc., are done in the same rhythm. You will need to cue the audience on their lines at first, but they will soon catch on and respond to your chant. You can add obstacles to this tale and stretch it out as long as you like. Go in and out of ditches, through mud wallows, over mountains. Invent sound effects and actions for each. Another fun way to use this story is to let the audience members call out obstacles and lead the story briefly. You all keep leg slapping and marching until someone comes up with another obstacle—"Oh, LOOK!" The member who calls out the obstacle also invents the sound effects and motion to get you through it.

# Drawing Stories

A drawing story is a handy thing to know. All you need is a pencil and paper. You can entertain a child quietly with a story sketched and whispered in the ear. Then pass over the pencil and paper and let the child draw the story. This is a good activity to quiet a child while traveling or in a crowded waiting room.

Here is a drawing story from Kenya.

## THE STORK

There once was a man who lived in a round little house.
His house had a round little window.
His house had a long triangular garden out in front.

(*Drawing.*) Ve-e-e-e-ry long.

Not far from this man's house there was a pond.
That pond had many fish in it.

(*Drawing.*) Just LOOK at all of these fish!

One night the man was awakened by a terrible noise:
SHUUUUU . . . SHUUUUU . . . SHUUUUU . . .

He jumped out of his bed and ran down to the pond
to see what could be the matter.

He saw nothing at the pond, so he ran right around the
pond . . .
and down a path on the other side of the pond . . .
looking for the trouble.
BLONK!
That man fell over a big boulder
sitting right in the middle of the path.
He picked himself up and ran on . . .

SPLUNCH!
That poor man fell into a DITCH.
He climbed right out, and
SPLUNCH!
he fell into another ditch.
He climbed out of THAT ditch, and
SPLUNCH!
he fell into ANOTHER ditch.

"Ups and downs.
Ups and downs.
This is useless," said the man.

At last he stopped and listened.
He could still hear that noise:
SHUUUUU . . . SHUUUUU . . . SHUUUUU . . .
"Oh, dear!
The noise is coming from the other direction!"

The man hurried back up to the pond.

He continued around the pond
and started down a second path.

        BLONK!

He fell over another big boulder.
On he ran.

        SPLUNCH!

Into another DITCH.
Out again.

        SPLUNCH!

In again.
Out again.

        SPLUNCH!

In AGAIN.
The poor man pulled himself out of the last ditch.

He hung his head and
went back toward the pond.

"Ups and downs.
Ups and downs.
This is hopeless."

But when the man reached the pond, he heard the
sound again:

      SHUUUUU . . . SHUUUUU . . . SHUUUUU . . .

This time it was very close.
The sound was coming from the end of the pond!
The man rushed over, and
THERE WAS THE CAUSE!

The dam at the end of the pond had broken.
The water was rushing out
and carrying the fishes with it!
Quickly the man worked to stop up the dam.

At last it was done, and the poor, tired man
dragged himself home and went back to bed.
"Ups and downs.
Ups and downs.
What a terrible day," said the man.

But in the morning when he awoke,
he looked out his window,
and what did he see? . . .

A lovely STORK!
"Oh," he said, laughing.
"Perhaps all those ups and downs
were worth it after all."

For more drawing stories and other entertaining stories using objects and paper folding,
see the list on page 108.

# Scary Stories

# Telling Terrifying Tales

Older children love scary stories; usually the creepier the stories are, the better the children like them. Second-grade boys pass these tales among themselves. A night of silent eavesdropping at any Scout overnight would give you a sizable repertoire of scary stories. And frankly, these kids are the best source for such tales. This type of folklore is constantly changing and being reinvented in contemporary form. When looking for spooky tales to tell, consider four types of material:

- Traditional folktales. Your public library probably contains many collections that include traditional folktales about people who encounter ghosts, goblins, and other monsters. Many of these tales have exciting story lines and can be made quite scary through your telling style. Because they are *only* stories, they do not tend to leave a permanent fright with the child.

- Jump tales. The two tales given here are samples of this type of tale. The teller leads the audience on, going into a haunted house, up stairs, or down into a basement step by step. At the tale's end, the teller yells *"Boo!"* and *jumps* at the audience. This type of tale is effective if told with the lights dimmed. The story should be drawn out eerily, and the jump at the end has to come quite unexpectedly to achieve the desired effect.

- Urban legends. One of the most active forms of contemporary folklore is the *urban legend*. These are essentially ghastly rumors. No one is ever able to trace them to an actual event, but everyone hears about them. The case of the vanishing hitchhiker is one of the more famous urban legends. Driving along a lonely road late at night, a man stops to pick up a young woman. When he stops later to let her out, she vanishes. He describes her to someone in the next town, and she is identified as a young woman who died years ago at the very spot where he picked her up.

    Folklorist Jan Harold Brunvand has written four collections of such material.

These are suitably spooky for telling to older children and teens. Because they are told as true happenings, these are more frightening than simple folktales and jump stories. A list of Brunvand's urban-legend books is on page 109.

- Local ghost legends. Most frightening of all are tales of the supernatural that are believed to be true. Every place has local legends of ghostly events. Adults elaborate these to scare children at campouts. Because these are believed by some to refer to actual supernatural happenings, this material is potentially very frightening to children.

## Setting the Scene for a Spooky Event

Decide in advance just how scary you want your tellings to be. The same story can be made gently amusing or truly terrifying, depending on its telling. For younger children select less frightening tales and tell them with an eye on your audience's response, so you can soften the tale if younger listeners seem frightened.

For older listeners set the stage with a darkened room lit only by candle or firelight. Speak in hushed and shivery tones, implying that this story scares even *you!* Now is the time to pull out the stops on your storytelling histrionics.

## Two Jump Tales

Here are patterns for two scary stories. You can make them as long and frightening as you like through your elaboration. To create a really spine-tingling effect, pretend they took place in the dark, dark spot where you are actually telling the story.

### THE DARK, DARK HOUSE

In a dark, dark house, there was a dark, dark stair.
Up the dark, dark stair, there was a dark, dark hall.
Down the dark, dark hall, there was a dark, dark door.
Behind the dark, dark door, there was a dark, dark room.
In the dark, dark room, there was a dark, dark closet.
In the dark, dark closet, there was a dark, dark box.
In the dark, dark box, there was a dark, dark hand!
And the dark, dark hand, said . . . "GOTCHA!"

**When Telling "The Dark, Dark House."** Tell this in a very serious, slow tone, building the suspense. On the last line slowly raise your hand; then on the "GOTCHA!" grab your listener.

## THE COFFIN

A popular tale for scary campfire telling is "The Coffin." A coffin is heard on the stairs; it is heard in the hall. The story can follow the pattern of "The Dark, Dark House" above, or it can be elaborated as the coffin pursues the teller into the woods, down tunnels, and so on. The story ends when the pursued person stops and shouts, "ENOUGH. TAKE THIS!" and gives it a Vicks: Then "The coughin' stops."

Though this is really just a corny joke, it can be very effective when elaborated in a spooky fashion. I have heard it told in a twenty-minute version that had a pack of Cub Scouts on the edge of their seats. The laugh at the end relieves the tension of the scary build-up.

Try your hand at scaring the daylights out of your kids with these two jump tales. Then look through the books listed under "Scary Stories," pages 109, for more scary stories to share.

## The Scary Story: To Tell or Not to Tell?

In *The Uses of Enchantment: The Meaning and Importance of Fairy Tales*, Bruno Bettelheim talks about the value of the folktale as a vehicle through which a child can work out his or her own fears. Through shared stories, children realize that they are not alone in their nightmares. And by identifying with the hero or heroine, the child learns that seemingly insurmountable odds and horrifying monsters can be overcome. You will want to make up your own mind about the use of frightening stories and violent tales of monsters, but you may find Bettelheim's ideas worth examining.

# Jokes
# as Stories

# Humor as a Starting Point

Simple jokes can sometimes be elaborated into good stories. Keep your ears open for humorous material that you might rework for your children's enjoyment. Although we often hear great jokes that have potential for retelling, the buildup to the punch line is sometimes told in a form that is either too brief to be a good story or too elaborate for easy retelling. These great jokes can be adapted into funny stories with just a little work.

As an example, here is a story that I first heard as an adult joke. It seemed to have potential as an enjoyable children's story, so I reworked it slightly and began sharing it with children.

## THE BIG-MOUTH FROG

There once was a little frog with a VERY BIG MOUTH.
That frog used to drive everybody crazy with his big mouth.
He was always opening it and hollering at people.
"HI! WHO ARE YOU?
I'M THE BIG-MOUTH FROG!"

One morning he decided to find out
what everybody ate for breakfast.
He hopped out of his frog pond,

hopped up to the zoo,
and began to pester all the animals.

The first animal he met was the giraffe.
"HI! WHO ARE YOU?
WHAT DO YOU EAT FOR BREAKFAST?"
The giraffe looked down.
"I am the GIRAFFE.
I eat leaves for breakfast."
"I'M THE BIG-MOUTH FROG!"
I EAT FLIES FOR BREAKFAST!"
He stuck out his long tongue, and SLUUURP, he caught a fly.

The big-mouth frog went to visit the elephant.
"HI! WHO ARE YOU?
WHAT DO YOU EAT FOR BREAKFAST?"
"I am the ELEPHANT.
I eat leaves for breakfast."
"I'M THE BIG-MOUTH FROG!"
I EAT FLIES FOR BREAKFAST!"
He stuck out his long tongue, and SLUUURP, he caught a fly.

The big-mouth frog went to visit the crocodile.
"HI! WHO ARE YOU?
WHAT DO YOU EAT FOR BREAKFAST?"
"I am the CROCODILE.
I eat BIG-MOUTH FROGS for breakfast.
Who did you say you were?"
"I'M THE BIG-MOUTH— Oops!
I'm the SMALL-mouth frog.
I eat FL— Oops . . .
MO-O-SQUI-I-TO-O-ES for breakfast."

And that small-mouth frog hopped right back to his pond.
OOOH . . . OOOH. (*His mouth is making a tiny "o."*)

And sat on his lily pad.

OOOH . . . OOOH.

And never opened his big mouth again.

**When Telling "The Big-Mouth Frog."**   The success of this story hinges on your facial antics. Open your mouth very wide when the big-mouth frog talks and speak in a very loud voice. When he decides he'd better become a small-mouth frog, purse your lips tightly and use a tiny voice.

**Adapting a Joke or Story for Telling**.   Now let's take a look at a joke version of the big-mouth frog story and see how I adapted it for telling as a children's story:

> A big-mouth frog goes to the zoo and hops into the lion's cage. And he says, "Hello, Mrs. Lion! I'm a big-mouth frog. What do you feed your babies?" *(Spoken with mouth widely extended.)* Mrs. Lion says, "Go on, get out of here. I don't have time for you." And so he hops out into the tiger's cage and says, "Hello, Mrs. Tiger. I'm a big-mouth frog. What do you feed your babies?" And Mrs. Tiger says, "Go on, go 'way." So he hops into the alligator cage and says, "Hello, Mrs. Alligator! I'm a big-mouth frog. What do you feed your babies?" "Big-mouth frogs." "Oh, really?" *(Spoken with lips pursed and brow furrowed in sudden sincerity.)*

To elaborate this into a story, I add a bit more dialogue between the big-mouth frog and the animals. I repeat the conversations in exactly the same way every time the frog meets another animal. Children enjoy this repetition, and it allows them to join you on the refrains if they like: "I'M THE BIG-MOUTH FROG!"

Some tellers are adept at adding elaborate description and asides to their stories. If you are good at this, by all means indulge your talents. I enjoy a simple retelling myself, and find this easier for beginning tellers to work with.

Keep your audience in mind as you plan your retelling. Knowing that I would be telling "The Big-Mouth Frog" to very young children, I elaborated the ending a bit. The joke at the story's end, in which the frog suddenly changes his mouth size, is not immediately clear to small children. So I elaborated the ending to give it a satisfying conclusion for them. For an older audience the story ends successfully with the frog's puckered "Oh. I'm the small-mouth frog."

# Family Stories

# Tales from Your Own Childhood

Storytelling can be as simple as the recounting of your own childhood experiences. These can be the most important stories you tell to your children. They learn from these stories about your childhood feelings and your attempts to cope with the same sort of problems they cope with today. Children find this type of story immensely useful. And these need not be stories of exciting adventures. The simple stories of going to the store for candy or picking peaches with Grandpa may be the best loved.

To get started with this personal storytelling, it will help if you sit down and make a list. Think over the things you recall from your childhood. Which would you enjoy sharing with your children? Jot these down and refer to this list of favorite remembrances when you need more fuel for your storytelling fire.

# Stories About Your Family

Maybe you are one of those lucky people who heard stories while you were growing up. If so, you will want to pass those tales on to your own children. Your first reaction may be, No one told stories to *me*. But stop and think about it. Didn't your great-aunt Hilda tell you stories of the one-room school where she used to teach? Remember that story about Uncle Ned and the cow? And what about Grandpa's Model T story? Most folks have many such family stories. These need to be passed on to the next generation. They are part of your family history. And they are great fun to hear, besides.

Each of us can make his or her own list of such tales. These are the tales that record our family history. They are important in bonding families and in giving our children a sense of family identity. In order to be sure and share these gems with your children, you will want to make a list. Jot them down as they come to mind. Recheck your list as your children grow, to make sure you keep telling these tales. You don't want your children to miss out on hearing the great stories from their own family heritage.

Here is an example from my own family.

## GRANDPA AND THE BLACKSNAKE

When Grandpa Garfield was a young man,
he went courting my Grandma Ella.
Now in those days down in Southern Indiana where he lived,
the teenage boys had a strange way of showing off their strength.

If a kid could find a big old blacksnake
stretched out by the fence row sunning itself,
he would sneak up on it from behind . . .
grab that blacksnake by the tail . . .
and whip it around his head like a blacksnake whip!
Then when he had it whirling real good . . .
he would CRACK that snake . . . just like a whip.
And if he was strong enough . . .
why, that blacksnake's head would snap right off.
Well, one Saturday night Grandpa was going down
across the field to Grandma's house.
He was all dressed up in his best shirt,
feeling real proud of himself.
Grandpa saw the tail of a snake sticking out of the grass.
He couldn't resist.
Just grabbed that tail and yanked that old snake out of that grass.
Began whirling it around over his head.
CRACKED that snake just like a whip.
But it backfired.
That snake backlashed and came wrapping right around his neck.

Grandpa thought he was a goner for sure.
He didn't know if he'd managed to snap that snake head off or not.
Suddenly he realized he hadn't even checked
to make sure it was a blacksnake.
It might have been a poisonous copperhead . . . or a moccasin. . . .
Grandpa just about fainted with fright.
Then he looked down.
He had snapped the head off that snake, all right.
And the blood was gushing down the front of his clean white shirt.

Grandpa had to go home and change his clothes
before he could go and see Grandma that night.
Now, that is a true story.
They really did things like that back in those days.

To make this simple anecdote into a story, I framed the tale by telling the audience when and where it took place: "When Grandpa . . . went courting . . . down in Southern Indiana." I explained the custom of blacksnake cracking to set up the story. It might have been useful to include an aside about the nature of blacksnake whips too; those long leather whips used in working horses looked a lot like blacksnakes and were known as "blacksnake whips." Knowing that might help the imagery of the story. Try to note any old customs important to your story for which your children will need explanation, and clear these up before you launch into the action.

In telling this, I try to imagine how Grandpa must have felt and try to visualize just how the action might have looked. Use your own memory of the relative whose story you are telling and the knowledge of the locale to flesh out your story.

For this story I use the Southern Indiana speech patterns of my own family. If you can remember the way your relatives spoke, or recall exact phrases from their tellings, try to fit these into your story.

I closed this with the traditional claim that this is a *true* story. And I refer once again to this story as one from the old days. This kind of closing gives the story a feeling of completion. By framing the story with such specific openings and closings, I give the simple anecdote the feel of a complete tale.

Of course it is not necessary to *plan* your tellings of these family stories at all, unless you want to. Just start telling your children the things you remember, and chances are you will automatically do all the things I mentioned above. The important thing is to share the remembrances. To help you think about writing down your family stories, see "Books to Take You Further," especially page 109.

# Folklore from Your Family

Every family has its own bits of folklore. We have family sayings, family jokes, family stories, special ways of doing things. These things give us a sense of identity. They remind us that we are a group, that we share common remembrances. You will want to pass some of these along to your children. As you did with your family stories, you may want to start a notebook of family sayings, family jokes, family traditions.

My father has a saying for almost every situation. And there is always a story to explain the saying, if I ask to hear it. Many of them are local stories from our Southern Indiana home; others are contemporary jokes. But once he latches onto them and begins to use them to point up situations in our family life, they tend to stick and become "family sayings."

On the small island where my parents now live, an annual Labor Day Rummage Sale is held to make money for the Community Hall. One Sunday at dinner my mom was discussing the rummage she planned to take. The year before, she had bought at the rummage sale a brand-new toaster that failed to work. "I think I might just donate it back," she said. "Might as well," quipped my ninety-year-old father. "What they don't know won't hurt them." Everyone at the table laughed at that, because we all knew the story of the rat in the cream jar.

Here is the way my dad tells it:

## THE RAT IN THE CREAM JAR

This was a woman who churned her own butter.
And one time the rats got into her cream jar.
She always kept the cream
in a big jar down the cellar with the lid on,
and of course somebody forgot to put the lid back on
and a rat got in there.
She went down and found a rat . . .
a dead rat . . .
in her cream jar.

Course she didn't want to throw all that cream away.
So she just churned it into butter.
Took that butter into the grocery store where she did her trading.

Takes it in to the grocer and just sneaks up to one side to one ear
and tells him,
"Now, I churned this and a rat got in my cream jar . . .
but I didn't want to throw it all away.
So . . . I just churned it up into butter.
And I'd like you to give me a pound of *good* butter
to take back home with me.
You can sell *that* to somebody else."
She says, "What they don't know won't hurt them."

Sure, he could do that all right.
So she went on to town to do her shopping at the other stores.
Come back after a while.
He had it all wrapped up, you know.
And he give it to her.
She thought it was somebody else's good butter.
But he had just wrapped her own butter up
and given it back to her.
He said, "What she don't know won't hurt her."

94

Whenever we catch somebody trying to pass something off falsely, my father tells the story of the rat in the butter. Or sometimes he just says, "That's like the old lady with the rat in her cream jar," and we all laugh because we already *know* the story. You probably have similar stories in your family. If you take the time to jot them down as you remember them or hear them, you may end up with a nice set of "Grandpa's stories" to pass on to your children.

I kept a record of the stories my father was telling for several months, then sat him down with a tape recorder and asked him to tell some of them again. I provided him with a good audience of listeners for this tape-recorded session, because most tellers are livelier and more inventive when encouraged by an audience.

Start your list of family stories right now and keep adding to it whenever something reminds you of another great family tale. For more examples of family folklore, see p. 109.

# Stories You Create

# Stories About Your Child

A simple storytelling event that needs to be repeated often is the recounting in story format of happenings from your child's own life. Even a very simple remembering of the events of the day can be useful to the child in making sense of his or her life. Begin simply: "Once there was a little girl named Julie. One Saturday morning Julie woke up and smelled something good in the air. Julie jumped out of bed and ran to the kitchen calling, 'Mommie! Mommie! *Bacon!'*" This kind of telling can be as long or as short as you like.

Retelling the events of the child's day at bedtime helps the child revisit the problems or pleasures of the day and remember or resolve them. You may want to end this telling with the same reassuring ending each time. "So Julie climbed into bed, and Daddy tucked her in and said, 'Good night, Julie. Sleep tight.' And Julie said, 'Good night, Daddy,' and closed her eyes and fell asleep."

This is the simplest sort of storytelling, and it never fails to be pleasing and useful to the child.

## Tales of the Imaginary Other Child

Another technique for helping your child cope through storytelling is the telling of a story about an imaginary child who is encountering problems just like those your child is facing. If your young son fears visiting a friend who owns a large, overactive dog, tell a story of a boy who visits a home with a huge dog and copes with its unwanted lunges and licks. Let your child help create these stories by telling you the way the child in the story feels and by offering possible solutions to that child's problem.

Australian psychologist Doris Brett has written about the "Annie Story," an imaging technique she has devised to help the child solve his or her own problems through guided imagery in storytelling. See the reading list on p. 109.

# Tales from Your Own Imagination

When I talk with parents who regularly use stories, they often speak excitedly about the fun they have making up stories for their children. Often a favorite fantasy character emerges through many tellings. The parent develops more and more episodes of the character's marvelous adventures. This delightful legacy of fantasy may remain in your children's imaginations and be passed on to *their children* in turn.

One hint for those who launch into their own fanciful adventures: It might be wise to have a stock of plausible endings in mind before you start. A Fijian friend, Pio Manoa, has a great trick for ending any story that begins to run too long. He just kills the hero off in battle! Pio says that is a great ending because in Fijian tradition it means the hero will live in memory forever. That trick might not work with *your* audience, but a similar stock ending could prove useful. Give some thought to whether you want your story's protagonist to marry and live happily ever after, find a treasure and live richly ever after, or just come home, climb into bed, and reflect on a fine adventure.

Some parents use their imaginations to adapt favorite tales in playful new ways. One technique used by parents and child-care providers is that of putting the child in the story. The Gingerbread Man bumps into David! Another technique involves re-setting the story in an environment familiar to the child. One nanny, Nat Whitman, tells of keeping his three-year-old charge entertained for an hour with a telling of "The Little Red Hen" reset in their vacation spot, Tenerife! These techniques of adding immediacy to the tale are most often used with very young children as a device for holding their attention and drawing them into the story.

If you enjoy this kind of imagination play, by all means employ it in your storytelling. But do not feel intimidated if this free-form approach to storytelling is not your cup of tea. The warmth of sharing and the joint entry into a magical world are the things that make storytelling so delightful . . . whether the story is an old tale retold or a fanciful new adventure.

# Tales from Your Child's Imagination

Once you have set a pattern of storytelling for your children, they will want to begin creating stories of their own. Make time to listen as well as to tell. A shared storytelling session, in which you hear their tellings, can prove a fascinating window into the inner worlds of your children.

This story creation allows the child to exercise his or her growing imagination. And the act of relating the tales helps the child learn to structure story and to speak it aloud.

To start the child on the storytelling path, you may want to try these activities:

**Create a Tale in Tandem**. Try creating a story together. You start the story. When you reach a certain point, stop . . . and let your child invent the tale from there. The child can stop at any time and hand the storytelling back to you. Older children love this and sometimes make it into a contest, getting their protagonist into some horrid situation and then turning the story back to you to see how you solve the tale.

Your first attempts at this may be hesitant, but both you and your child will grow in skill if you play storytelling games regularly.

**Traveling on the Story Cloud**. My neighbor, Pat Hill, created a charming imagination play for her family. Pat places all the children on an imaginary Story Cloud. Then she sails them over a varying landscape. Pat describes the things they see below, and whenever they pass a place that strikes one child's fancy, that child jumps in and takes over the story. When Pat passes them over a train, for example, Taylor may jump in with an exciting story of train wrecks and daring rescues. When Taylor begins to lag in his narrative, Pat loads them all back onto the cloud and sails off in search of other magical sites, or passes the tale to another eager teller.

**The Story Ball**.  Sit in a circle with your children and begin telling a story. Hold a ball in your hand. When you reach the point at which you want to pass the story on, just toss the ball to the teller you choose to tell next. The tellers keep passing the ball from person to person as the story unfolds.

**The Story Yarn**.  This story game works best with a small group. It is a variant on the story ball, but requires more skill. The players sit on the floor and roll a ball of yarn from teller to teller. Each holds on to the yarn string as the ball moves on. At the end a story web has been woven in the circle's center. After everyone has been incorporated into the story, begin unweaving the story web. As the tellers' order reverses, the tale winds down. The tale should end when the ball is completely rewound.

These are start-up activities only. Once the children learn to access the imagination, you can abandon the game format and encourage them to fabricate stories. The main requirement for this imaginative storytelling is a parent who takes the time to listen.

# More Tales and Tellers

At the end of this book is a list of story collections and books about storytelling. These will give you many more good tales to share. You might also want to listen to audio- and videotapes of professional storytellers. The children's librarian at your public library will be glad to suggest more story material.

For inspiration, you may want to take your family to hear other tellers. Check the events calendar in your local newspaper for storytelling events. Far from being a dead art form, storytelling is very much alive in the world today. Hundreds of professional storytellers tour the world, sharing their art. Educators, librarians, ministers, recreation leaders, health-care providers, and others use storytelling in their work.

In many areas tellers network through storytelling guilds, which offer performances, workshops, and story swaps. For lists of storytelling guilds, see *The Storytelling Directory*. It is published annually by the National Storytelling Network. This directory also lists festivals, workshops, and storytelling classes; contains a directory of professional story-tellers; and includes a list of storytelling resources.

The National Storytelling Network, formerly known as the National Association for the preservation and Perpetuation of Storytelling, has over 7,000 members. Its journal,

*Storytelling Magazine*, contains articles about storytelling, news of the storytelling world, and good tales for telling. Ask for *Storytelling Magazine* at your library or write to the National Storytelling Network for membership information.

The National Storytelling Network
116 West Main Street
Jonesborough, TN 37659
1-800-525-4514
nsn@naxs.net
www.storynet.org

# Books to Take You Further

Here are some of my own favorite stories for telling, and other books to help you tell stories. Your children's librarian will be delighted to suggest more.

## Books to Help Improve Your Storytelling Skills

*Just Enough to Make a Story*, by Nancy Schimmel (Berkeley, CA: Sisters' Choice, 1992).

*The Storyteller's Start-Up Book*, by Margaret Read MacDonald (Little Rock: August House, 1993).

*Tell Me Another: Storytelling and Reading Aloud at Home, at School and in the Community*, by Bob Barton (Markham, Ontario: Pembroke, 1986).

*The Way of the Storyteller*, by Ruth Sawyer (New York: Viking, 1962).

## Familiar Nursery Tales

*Chimney Corner Stories: Tales for Little Children*, by Veronica S. Hutchinson (Hamden, CT: Linnet, 1992).

*Great Children's Stories: The Classic Volland Edition*, by Frederick Richardson (Chicago: Rand McNally, 1972).

*The Fairy Tale Treasury*, by Virginia Haviland, illus. by Raymond Briggs (New York: Coward McCann, 1972).

*The Helen Oxenbury Nursery Story Book*, by Helen Oxenbury (New York: Knopf, 1985).

*The Three Bears & 15 Other Stories*, by Anne Rockwell (New York: Harper, 1975).

*The Three Little Pigs and Other Favorite Nursery Stories*, by Charlotte Voake (Cambridge, MA: Candlewick, 1992).

## Fingerplays

*Creative Fingerplays and Action Rhymes: an Index and Guide to Their Use,* by Jeff Defty (Phoenix: Oryx, 1992).

*Games for the Very Young: A Treasury of Nursery Songs and Finger Plays,* by Elizabeth Matterson (New York: American Heritage, 1969). (Also published as *This Little Puffin,* New York: Penguin, 1969.)

*Here's a Ball for Baby: Finger Rhymes for Young Children,* by Jenny Williams (New York: Dial, 1987).

## Stories with Audience-Participation Possibilities

*Joining In: An Anthology of Audience Participation Stories and How to Tell Them,* by Teresa Miller (Cambridge, MA: Yellow Moon, 1988). Stories contributed by sixteen professional storytellers.

*Look Back and See: Twenty Lively Tales for Gentle Tellers,* by Margaret Read MacDonald (New York: Wilson, 1991).

*Shake-It-Up Tales!: Stories to sing, Dance, Drum, and Act Out,* by Margaret Read MacDonald (Little Rock: August House, 2000).

*The Singing Sack: 28 Song Stories from Around the World,* by Helen East (London: A&C Black, 1989).

*Twenty Tellable Tales: Audience Participation Folktales for the Beginning Storyteller,* by Margaret Read MacDonald (New York: Wilson, 1986).

## Multicultural Folktales for the Storyteller

*Celebrate the World: Twenty Tellable Folktales for Multicultural Festivals,* by Margaret Read MacDonald (New York: Wilson, 1994).

*Grandfather Tales,* by Richard Chase (Boston: Houghton Mifflin, 1948).

*Lion and Ostrich Chicks, and Other African Folk Tales,* by Ashley Bryan (New York: Atheneum, 1986).

*The Magic Orange Tree and Other Haitian Folktales,* by Diane Wolkstein (New York: Knopf, 1978).

*Songs and Stories from Uganda,* by Moses Serawadda (New York: Crowell, 1974).

## Comparing Folktale Variants

These books contain several variants of one folktale, for comparison purposes.

*Beauties and Beasties: Oryx Multicultural Folktale Series,* by Betsy Hearne (Phoenix: Oryx, 1993).

*Cinderella: Oryx Multicultural Folktale Series,* by Judy Sierra (Phoenix: Oryx, 1992).

*A Knock on the Door: Oryx Multicultural Folktale Series,* by George Shannon (Phoenix: Oryx, 1992).

*Tom Thumb: Oryx Multicultural Folktale Series,* by Margaret Read MacDonald (Phoenix: Oryx, 1992).

## Story Stretches

*Crazy Gibberish: Story Time Stretches,* by Naomi Baltuck (Hamden, CT: Linnet, 1992).

*Juba This and Juba That: Story Hour Stretches for Large or Small Groups,* by Virginia Tashjian (Boston: Little, Brown, 1969).

## Drawing Stories

*The Family Storytelling Handbook: How to Use Stories, Anecdotes, Rhymes, Handkerchiefs, Paper, and Other Objects to Enrich Your Family Traditions,* by Anne Pellowski (New York: Macmillan, 1987).

*The Story Vine: A Source Book of Unusual and Easy-to-Tell Stories from Around the World,* by Anne Pellowski (New York: Macmillan, 1984).

## Scary Stories

*Scary Stories to Tell in the Dark: Collected from Folklore,* by Alvin Schwartz (New York: Lippincott, 1981).

*More Scary Stories to Tell in the Dark,* collected from folklore and retold by Alvin Schwartz (New York: Harper, 1984).

*The Thing at the Foot of the Bed and Other Scary Tales,* by Maria Leach (Cleveland: World, 1959).

*When the Lights Go Out: 20 Scary Tales to Tell,* by Margaret Read MacDonald (New York: Wilson, 1988).

## Urban Legend

*The Choking Doberman and Other "New" Urban Legends,* by Jan Harold Brunvand (New York: Norton, 1984).

*Curses! Broiled Again!: The Hottest Urban Legends Going,* by Jan Harold Brunvand (New York: Norton, 1989).

*The Mexican Pet,* by Jan Harold Brunvand (New York: Norton, 1986).

*The Vanishing Hitchhiker: American Urban Legends and Their Meanings,* by Jan Harold Brunvand (New York: Norton, 1981).

## Stories and Activities for Nature Walks

*Hidden Stories in Plants: Unusual and Easy-to-Tell Stories from Around the World Together with Creative Things to Do While Telling Them,* by Anne Pellowski (New York: Macmillan, 1990).

*Keepers of the Earth: Native American Stories and Environment Activities for Children,* by Michael J. Caduto and Joseph Bruchac (Golden, CO: Fulcrum, 1988).

## Stories to Make You Think

*Aesop's Fables,* by Fulvio Testa (New York: Barron, 1989).

*Earth Care: World Folktales to Talk About,* by Margaret Read MacDonald (Hamden, CT: Linnet, 1999).

*Peace Tales: World Folktales to Talk About,* by Margaret Read MacDonald (Hameden, CT: Linnet, 1992).

*Stories for Telling: A Treasury for Christian Storytellers,* by William R. White (Minneapolis: Augsburg, 1986).

## Telling Family Stories

*Annie Stories: A Special Kind of Storytelling,* by Doris Brett (New York: Workman, 1986).

*A Celebration of American Family Folklore: Tales and Traditions from the Smithsonian Collection,* by Steven J. Zeitlin, Amy J. Kotkin, and Holly Cutting Baker (New York: Pantheon, 1982).

*Families Writing,* by Peter R. Stillman (Cincinnati: Writer's Digest Books, 1989).

*The Family Storytelling Handbook: How to Use Stories, Anecdotes, Rhymes, Handkerchiefs, Paper, and Other Objects to Enrich Your Family Traditions,* by Anne Pellowski (New York: Macmillan, 1987).

*Telling Your Own Stories,* by Donald Davis (Little Rock: August House, 1993).

## Riddle Stories

Tell the story. Let the audience guess the answer.

*Stories to Solve: Folktales from Around the World,* by George Shannon (New York: Greenwillow, 1985).

*More Stories to Solve,* by George Shannon (New York: Greenwillow, 1990).

*Still More Stories to Solve,* by George Shannon (New York: Greenwillow, 1994).

## Picture Book Sources

Using folktale picture books (J398 at your library) can be a good way to expand your telling repertoire. Here is a brief sampling.

*Baby Rattlesnake*, told by Te Ata, adapted by Lynn Moroney (San Francisco: Children's Book Press, 1989).

*The Old Woman Who Lived in a Vinegar Bottle*, by Margaret Read MacDonald (Little Rock: August House, 1995).

## Favorite Stories of Professional Tellers

*Homespun: Tales from America's Favorite Storytellers*, by Jimmy Neil Smith (New York: Crown, 1988).

*Ready-to-Tell Tales: Sure-Fire Stories from America's Favorite Storytellers*, edited by David Holt and Bill Mooney (Little Rock: August House, 1994).

*More Ready-to-Tell Tales from Around the World*, edited by David Holt and Bill Mooney (Little Rock: August House, 2000).

## To Locate a Tale Whose Title You Know, Stories on a Certain Subject, or to Find Several Variants of One Tale

*Index to Fairy Tales, 1978–1986: Including Folklore, Legends, and Myths in Collections*, by Norma Olin Ireland and Joseph w. Sprug (Metuchen, NJ: Scarecrow, 1989). See also its earlier editions.

*The Storyteller's Sourcebook: A Subject, Title, and Motif-Index to Folklore Collections for Children*, by Margaret Read MacDonald (Detroit: Gale Research/Neal-Schuman, 1981).

*The Storyteller's Sourcebook 1983–1999*, by Margaret Read MacDonald and Brian Sturm (Detroit: Gale Research, 2001).

## Directory

*National Storytelling Directory*, by the National Storytelling Network (Jonesborough, TN). Annual.

# Tale Notes and Sources

The motif numbers mentioned in these notes refer to numbers assigned by *The Motif-Index of Folk-Literature*, by Stith Thompson, and an extension of that work, *The Storyteller's Sourcebook*, by Margaret Read MacDonald (noted with an asterisk).

## "The Three Bears"

Traditional English folktale. In an early version by Robert Southey, an old woman, rather than Goldilocks, enters the house. See: "Little Old Woman and Three Bears" in *English Folk and Fairy Tales*, by Joseph Jacobs (New York: Putnam, n.d.), pp. 96–101. Motif N831.1.2*, *Mysterious house intruder*.

## "The Little Red Hen"

Traditional English folktale. For an illustrated version see *Great Children's Stories*, by Frederick Richardson (Chicago: Rand McNally, 1972), pp. 9–15. Motif W111.6*, *The Little Red Hen and the grain of wheat*.

## "The Gingerbread Man"

Traditional European tale. For a Scandinavian version, in which a pig offers a ride over the river to a pancake, see *East of the Sun and West of the Moon*, by Peter Christen Asbjornsen and Jorgen Moe (New York: Row, Peterson, 1946), pp. 41–45. In a Scottish variant a wee bannock rolls down a fox's hole. Found in Joseph Jacobs, *More English Fairy Tales* (New York: Putnam, n.d.), pp. 73–77. Motif Z33.1, *The fleeing pancake*.

## "The Beehive"

Traditional fingerplay.

### "Foxie's Hole"

Traditional fingerplay.

### "The Parrot with the Key to Rome"

Simplified version of children's folk rhyme, with hand motions added. A Chilean version may be found in Oreste Plath, *Folklore Chileno* (Santiago: Editorial Nascimento, 1969), p. 244. Motif Z11, *Endless tale.*

### "The Lost Mitten"

The version offered here is expanded from a story in *Old Peter's Russian Tales*, by Arthur Ransome (New York: Nelson, 1916), pp. 228–30. A variant in which the animals set up house in the skull of a horse is found in *When the Lights Go Out*, by Margaret Read MacDonald (New York: Wilson, 1988), pp. 143–47. For a picture-book version see *The Mitten: A Ukrainian Folktale*, by Jan Brett (New York: Putnam, 1989). Motif J2199.5*, *Fools (usually animals) invite all comers to join them in abode until house ruptures.*

### "The Squeaky Door"

Adapted from "The Squeaky Bed," by New Zealand storyteller Elizabeth Miller, as recorded on her videotape *Folk Stories with Dreamweaver* (Invercargill, N.Z.: Rillstone & Associates, 1991). A Puerto Rican variant of this tale appears as "The Bed" in *The Tiger and the Rabbit and Other Tales*, by Pura Belpré (New York: Warne, 1932), pp. 32–35. Motif Z49.17*, *Little boy under bed given animals to comfort.*

### "Ms. Mouse Needs a Friend"

A brief version of this Siberian tale appears in *Animal Stories of the North: Kutkha the Raven*, illustrated by Y. Rachov, translated by Fainna Solasko (Moscow, Russia: Malysh Publishers, 1981), pp. 65–67. This tale reminds one of a tale popular in Spain, Latin America, and the Middle East in which a little cockroach or ant rejects all suitors. Motif Z32.3, *Little ant finds a penny, buys new clothes with it, and sits in her doorway. Various animals pass by and propose marriage.*

### "A Dark and Stormy Night"

This is elaborated from Motif Z17.2*: *"It was a dark and stormy night . . . the sailors began telling stories . . . 'It was a dark and stormy night.'"*

### "A Silly Question"

Elaborated from Motif Z17.1*, *"Once there was a girl who asked her father, 'What's a silly question?' and he replied, 'Once there was a girl who asked her father . . .'"*

### "The Bird Catcher"

Elaborated from Motif Z11.2, *Endless tale: Hundreds of birds in snare fly away one at a time.* For a good version of this story see *Toontoony Pie and Other Tales from Pakistan*, by Ashraf Siddiqui and Marilyn Lerch (Cleveland: World Publishing, 1961), pp. 155–57.

### "Cheese and Crackers"

This was elaborated from a brief tale in Leonard Roberts, *Old Greasybeard: Tales from the Cumberland*

*Gap* (Detroit: Folklore Associates, 1969), pp. 45–47. Roberts heard the story in 1954 from a teacher, Mrs. Minnie Shupe of Knox County, Kentucky. She heard it from a little girl in her classroom. Compare this story with "Sody Sallyrytus" in *Twenty Tellable Tales*, by Margaret Read MacDonald (New York: Wilson, 1986), pp. 79–89.

## "Strongest One of All"

Elaborated from a story found in *Folktales of the Amur: Stories from the Russian Far East*, by Dmitri Nagishkin (New York: Abrams, 1980), and in *The Sun Maid and the Crescent Moon: Siberian Folk Tales*, by James Riordan (New York: Interlink, 1989), pp. 112–12. See page 66 for four other versions of this tale. Motif Z42, *Stronger and strongest*. A similar tale is Motif L192, *Mouse stronger than wall*.

## "Let's Go on a Bear Hunt!"

This popular tale appears in many versions, as a lion hunt, witch hunt, ghost hunt. . . . Adapt it to fit your needs. The version given here is based on a group activity led by Robert Amick of Purdue University at an Amick family reunion in Scipio, Indiana, circa 1956.

For a Lion Hunt version see *Juba This and Juba That: Story Hour Stretches for Large or Small Groups*, by Virginia Tashjian (Boston: Little, Brown, 1969), pp. 62–70. For a Ghost Hunt see *When the Lights Go Out: 20 Scary Tales to Tell*, by Margaret Read MacDonald (New York: Wilson, 1988), p. 14.

## "The Stork"

This tale is retold from *The Bushbabies*, by William Stevenson (Boston: Houghton Mifflin, 1965), pp. 198–99. The novel is set in Kenya. A similar tale appears in *Out of Africa*, by Isak Dineson (New York: Random House, 1937), pp. 250–53.

## "The Dark, Dark House"

A traditional American tale. For another version see *The Thing at the Foot of the Bed*, by Maria Leach (Cleveland: World, 1959), p. 51. Motif Z13.1.4*. *Person enters dark, dark house, down dark, dark hall, etc. Ghost jumps out.*

## "The Coffin"

Elaborated from a jump tale told by a Cub Scout leader at Maywood Hills Elementary School in Bothell, Washington, November 1990.

## "The Big-Mouth Frog"

This story is elaborated from a joke cited in "The Curious Case of the Wide-Mouthed Frog" in *Interpreting Folklore*, by Alan Dundes (Bloomington, IN: Indiana University Press, 1980), pp. 12–16.

## "Grandpa and the Blacksnake"

Elaborated from a personal story told to Margaret Read MacDonald by her grandfather Parley Garfield Read in Jennings County, Indiana, circa 1954. Similar to tales appearing as Motif X1320, *Lies about reptiles*. However, this appears to be a true story, as blacksnake cracking was indeed common.

## "The Rat in the Cream Jar"

Quoted from " 'It Don't Take Long to Look at a Horseshoe': The Humorous Anecdote Catch-Phrase as Proverbial Saying," by Margaret Read MacDonald, in *Indiana Folklore and Oral History*, Vol. 15, No. 2, 1986, pp. 95–119. Told by Murray Read to his daughter in November 1974, Jennings County, Indiana.

# Index

Adapting stories, 85

African (Kenya) folktale, 71–73

American folktale, 67–70. *See also* Appalachian folktale

Anansi the Spider, values taught by, 3

"Annie Stories" (Brett), 100

Appalachian folktale, 53–61

Audience participation. *See also titles of specific stories*
    actions/activities, 66, 67, 70, 71
    chiming in on refrains, 11, 23
    how to encourage, 53
    responses to questions, 41
    sound effects, 41, 70
    sources for stories, 108

Babies
    stories for, 24–31
    telling stories to, 11

Bedtime rituals and storytelling, 5, 35
    "The Bird Catcher," 49
    ending your story, 10, 99
    expandable and endless tales, 25, 35, 48
    quieter telling of stories for, 11
    stories about your child, 99

"Beehive, The," 24, 111

Benefits of storytelling, 3–4

Bettelheim, Bruno, 79

"Big-Mouth Frog, The," 83–85, 113
    hints for telling, 85

"Bird Catcher, The," 49, 112

Bonding and storytelling, 4

Brett, Doris, 100

Brett, Jan, 31

Brunvand, Jan Harold, 77–78

Carpenter, Frances, 66

"Cheese and Crackers," 53–61, 112–13
    techniques for telling, 61
    tips for remembering, 61

Chilean tale, English and Spanish, 25–26

Chucha people of Siberia, folktale, 42–47

"Coffin, The," 79, 113

"Dark and Stormy Night, A," 48, 112

"Dark, Dark House, The," 78–79, 113
    hints for telling, 79

Drawing stories, 71
    sources for stories, 108
    "The Stork," 71–73

Educational benefits of storytelling
    developing imagination, 4, 103
    literary skills, 3–4
    oral skills, 4

Emotional development and storytelling, 4
    and fear of the dark, 35
    and scary stories, 79
    stories about the imaginary other child, 99–100

Ending your story
    at bedtime, 10
    closing phrases, 10
    morals, 47
    true stories, 92

Expandable and endless tales, 35, 42
    "A Dark and Stormy Night," 48
    "The Gingerbread Man, " 20–23
    "Ms. Mouse Needs a Friend," 42–47

"The Parrot with the Key to Rome," 25–26
"A Silly Question," 49
sources for stories, 108

Family and storytelling
    additional stories, 109
    developing sense of identity, 4, 35
    events to tell about, 9, 35, 89
    family folklore and family sayings, 93, 95
    "Grandpa and the Blacksnake," 90–91
    preserving family history, 3, 4, 90
    recording stories, 95
    strengthening ties, 4
    writing the stories down, 92
Fingerplay, 10–11, 24
    "The Beehive," 24
    "Foxie's Hole," 24
    "The Lost Mitten," 26–31
    "The Parrot with the Key to Rome," 25–26
    sources for, 108
Folktales
    "The Big-Mouth Frog," 83–85
    "The Bird Catcher," 49
    "Cheese and Crackers" (Appalachia), 53–61,
        112–13
    and emotional development, 4
    "Let's Go on a Bear Hunt" (American), 67–70,
        113
    "The Little Red Hen" (English), 18–19, 111
    "The Lost Mitten" (Russian), 26–31, 112
    "Ms. Mouse Needs a Friend" (Siberian), 42–47,
        112
    scary, 77
    "A Silly Question," 49
    sources for multicultural, 108
    "The Squeaky Door," 35–40
    "The Stork" (African), 71–73, 113
    "Strongest One of All" (Siberian), 62–66, 113
    "The Three Bears" (English), 1–18, 111
    variations from other countries, 66, 108
"Foxie's Hole," 24, 112
Friendship, story to teach about, 42–47

Games, storytelling, 103–4
Ghost stories, 78, 109
"Gingerbread Man, The," 20–23, 111
    hints on learning and telling, 9–10, 23
    individualizing, 21
    telling to very small children, 11
Gobhai, Mehli, 66
"Grandpa and the Blacksnake," 90–91, 113

"Henny Penny," 23
Hill, Pat, 103
Humor
    adapting jokes as stories, 83, 85
    "The Big-Mouth Frog," 83–85

Imagination, developing
    creating a tale in tandem, 103
    development of child's, 4, 103
    the story ball, 104
    the story yarn, 104
    tales from your own, 101–2
    traveling on the story cloud, 103
India, folktale from, 66
Indiana, story from, 92–93
Individualizing stories, 10, 101
    "The Gingerbread Man," 21, 101
    "Ms. Mouse Needs a Friend," 47
    stories about the imaginary other child, 99–100
    stories about your child, 35, 99
    stories about your family, 90, 92, 93, 95
    stories about your own childhood, 89

Japan, folktale from, 66
Jokes, as stories, 83–85. *See also* Humor
Jump tales, 77, 78
    "The Coffin," 79
    "The Dark, Dark House," 78–79

Kenya, story from, 71–73
Korea, folktale from, 66

Learning a story, suggestions, 9–10, 61

"Let's Go on a Bear Hunt," 67–70, 113
   hints for telling, 70
Listing stories to keep, 3
"Little Red Hen, The," 18–19, 111
   individualizing, 101
   repeated dialogue in, 19
"Little Red Riding Hood," 23
Locating certain stories, 110
"Lost Mitten, The," 26–31, 112
   hints for telling, 31
   Ukrainian version, 31, 112

Manoa, Pio, 101
McDermott, Gerald, 66
Miller, Elizabeth, 35
Mitten, The (Brett), 31
"Ms. Mouse Needs a Friend," 42–47, 112
   hints for telling, 47

Nanai people of eastern Siberia, folktale, 62–66
National Storytelling Association, 105–6
National Storytelling Directory, The, 105, 110
Nature walks, stories for, 109
Nursery tales, 15–23
   sources of, 107

Pakistan, folktales from, 49, 112
"Parrot with the Key to Rome, The," 25–26, 112

"Rat in the Cream Jar, The," 94–95, 114
Repetition, stories that stress
   "Cheese and Crackers," 53–61
   "The Little Red Hen," 19–20
   "The Gingerbread Man," 20–23
   "The Parrot with the Key to Rome," 25–26
Russian folktale, 26–31

Scary stories
   "The Coffin," 79
   "The Dark, Dark House," 78–79
   folktales, 77
   local ghost legends, 78
   jump tales, 77, 78
   setting the scene, 78
   sources for stories, 109
   urban legends, 77–78, 109
   the value in telling, 79
Siberia, folktales from, 42, 62
"Silly Question, A," 49, 112
Spanish-language story, 25–26
"Squeaky Door, The," 35–41, 112
   hints for telling, 41
Stone-Cutter, The (McDermott), 66
"Stork, The," 71–74
Story ball, 104
Storytellers, professional
   sources, 109
   where to find, 105–6
Storytelling Magazine, 106
Storytelling skills
   bounces and fingerplays, 10–11
   eye contact, 10
   individualizing stories, 10, 21
   marking key phrases, 10
   opening and closing phrases, 10
   setting the scene for a spooky story, 78
   showing mood changes, 10, 61
   sources to consult, 11, 107
   techniques, 11
   vocal expression, 9–10, 18, 61
Story yarn, 104
"Strongest One of All," 62–66, 113
   hints about telling, 66
   other versions, 66

Tales of a Korean Grandmother (Carpenter), 66
Techniques. See Storytelling skills
"Three Bears, The," 15–18, 111
"Three Billy Goats Gruff," 23
"Three Little Pigs, The," 23
Times for storytelling, suggestions, 4–5
Toad Is the Emperor's Uncle, The (Vo-Dinh), 66
Toddlers
   bounces and fingerplay for, 10–11

stories for, 24–31
telling stories to, 11
Traveling on the story cloud, 103

Urban legends, 77–78
sources for stories, 109
*Uses of Enchantment, The: The Meaning and
Importance of Fairy Tales* (Bettelheim), 79
*Usha the Mouse-Maiden* (Gobhai), 66

Values, using stories to teach, 3

friendship, 42–47
gluttony is bad, 3
sources for stories, 109
work ethic, 18–19
Variants, comparing folktales, 66, 108
Vietnam, folktale from, 66
Vo-Dinh, 66

Whitman, Nat, 101
Work ethic taught, 18–19

"During the telling of a story, the child and teller work as equals to breathe the story into personal life. With this, the child, forever dominated by the adult world, finds another element of joy: equality. The intimacy of the oral tradition fosters this creativity; though others may be physically present, the listening child creates as if in solitude."

—George Shannon, "Shared Treasures:
Folktales, Joy and the Listening Child as Artist"
in *The National Storytelling Journal*, Summer 1981

Along came a kitten
with a white snout.
And spit this little story out!